HURST'S WURST

Other books by Kevin D. McCann

Jackson Diamonds:
Professional Baseball in Jackson, Tennessee

The Peg-Legged Politician:
The Life of Adam Huntsman

The History of Liberty Church and School
McNairy County, Tennessee

The Correspondence, Speeches, and Writings
of Adam Huntsman

The McCanns of McNairy County, Tennessee:
The Descendants of John McCann Sr.

Adam Huntsman: West Tennessee Politician

HURST'S WURST

COLONEL FIELDING HURST
AND THE
SIXTH TENNESSEE CAVALRY U.S.A.

KEVIN D. MCCANN

McCann
PUBLISHING

McCann Publishing
204 Delaney Circle
Dickson, Tennessee 37055

ISBN-10: 0-9671251-2-X
ISBN-13: 978-0-9671251-2-1

Printed in the United States of America

McCann
PUBLISHING

To learn more about Fielding Hurst, the 6th Tennessee Cavalry, and other titles written by Kevin D. McCann, please visit his websites at www.kevindmccann.com and www.fieldinghurst.com

To the memories of my ancestors
who served in the 6th Tennessee Cavalry:

Cpl. John Wesley Plunk, Company G
Pvt. Mark M. Rose, Company A
Pvt. William Jasper Newton Rose, Company A

and to

Cindy, Braden, and Brianna
for their love and support

CONTENTS

Acknowledgements   iii

Preface   v

1. Forced To Choose Sides   1

2. A Nation Unto Himself   8

3. One Country, One Language, One Flag   17

4. Guerrillas In Their Midst   24

5. Such Wholesale and Wanton Destruction   35

6. A Field of More Active Operation   45

     Photographs   52

7. Grub Up West Tennessee   62

8. Run Like So Many Devils   70

9. Dismounted and Unassigned   76

10. This Seems Too Unequal   85

11. Epilogue   93

Appendices

Roster of the Sixth Tennessee Cavalry   97

Partial Casualty List from the Engagement at Bolivar, TN   117

Biographical Sketches of the Officers of the
Sixth Tennessee Cavalry   118

Samuel M. Meek Letter   127

Bibliography   131

Index   139

ACKNOWLEDGEMENTS

It was the discovery of a letter that sparked this fourth edition of *Hurst's Wurst* to be published. I am thankful to Colleen Holland for sending me the transcript of a letter in her possession describing the scene as Fielding Hurst was led a prisoner to the Corinth, Mississippi train station amid a throng of hecklers. For me, it shed light on one of many incidents that likely contributed to Hurst's vengeful actions against his secessionist neighbors during the Civil War.

A book may have a single author, but it is still a collaborative effort. Many people have made contributions both large and small over the past four editions of this book. First I would like to acknowledge three fellow historians who encouraged my research and writing efforts. I am grateful to Jack Darrel Wood and Robert Taylor, reference librarians of the Tennessee Room at the Jackson-Madison County Public Library in Jackson, Tennessee, for their encouragement over the years. Jack provided me with research materials he had collected about the Sixth Tennessee Cavalry that were invaluable to this work. I am also grateful to Jonathan K.T. Smith, whose local and regional publications were sources of inspiration to me as an undergraduate college student. He showed me that one did not need his work published by a large publishing company to share it with others. Dr. James Alex Baggett's History Seminar course at Union University taught me that local history is an interesting and worthwhile pursuit.

I would like to thank Derek Frisby for his generosity in sharing with me his dissertation entitled "'Homemade Yankees': West Tennessee Unionism in the Civil War Era." It is a scholarly and thorough account of the war in West Tennessee and the role of Unionists in it. He also took the time to track down a letter from Dew M. Wisdom to Colonel Philip D. Roddey that was essential to this edition.

There have been many others who have assisted me over the past twelve years, everything from sharing research and photos to offering encouragement in this endeavor. They include: Brad Borden, John Scott Kemp, Rickey Long, Judy Malone, L.M. McDaniel, Marilyn Rushing, John Sickles, Susie Carroll Summers, John E. Talbott, Ken Thacker, and Dr. Michael W. Thompson.

As always, I am grateful for the love and support of my wife Cindy and our two children, Braden and Brianna. They have blessed my life more than they will ever know.

Photographic Credits

Fielding Hurst (Brad Borden)
Lt. Col. William K.M. Breckenridge (John Sickles)
Brevet Brig. Gen. William J. Smith (Civil War Generals and Brevets)
Cpt. Nathan McDonald Kemp (John Scott Kemp)
Cpt. James L.W. Boatman (John Sickles)
Maj. Daniel M. Emerson (John Sickles)
Cpt. William Chandler (Dr. Michael W. Thompson)
Maj. Stanford L. Warren (*150 Years of Growth and Progress in McNairy County*)
Pvt. Pinkney W.H. Lee (John Sickles)
Cpl. James Richard Thacker (Ken Thacker)
Pvt. Wesley Parsons (Gordon Browning Museum and Genealogical Library)
1st Lt. John P. Gibbs (John Sickles)
Military Gov. Andrew Johnson (Library of Congress)
Gov. William G. Brownlow (Library of Congress)
Benjamin Henry Grierson (Civil War Generals and Brevets website)
Maj. Gen. Stephen A. Hurlbut (Library of Congress)
Nathan Bedford Forrest (Library of Congress)
Mason Brayman (Civil War Generals and Brevets website)
J. Willis Dodds tombstone (the author)
6th Tennessee Cavalry Reunion (L.M. McDaniel)
Company B, 6th Tennessee Cavalry (the author)
Romantic Adventure (*The Pictorial Book of Anecdotes and Incidents of the War of the Rebellion*)
USS Tyler (U.S. Naval Historical Center)
Fielding Hurst home (the author)
Staircase bullet crease (the author)
GAR Post No. 7 ribbon (John Scott Kemp)
Hurst Nation marker (the author)
Fielding Hurst tombstone (the author)

PREFACE

The Civil War is an integral part of the Southern heritage. There are reminders of the conflict everywhere from statues of Confederate soldiers on courthouse lawns and historical markers on highways to national military parks and cemeteries. Southerners are proud of their heritage; being from the South, they presume that their ancestors fought for the Confederacy and for Southern independence.

They might be surprised.

Not every brave son of the South fought against Northern aggression. Some took a different stand and defended the Stars and Stripes rather than take up the Stars and Bars. It meant placing their lives and those of their families in peril and withstanding verbal and physical persecution from their friends and neighbors. Approximately 31,092 Tennesseans fought in the Federal armies and an estimated 6,766 gave their lives for the Union. Twenty-five infantry regiments (including fourteen consisting of African-Americans), fifteen cavalry regiments, and eight mounted infantry regiments were organized in the state.[1] This is one of the lessons left out of most history books: contrary to popular belief, the South did not present an altogether united front; not every Southerner was a Rebel.

I love history, particularly Civil War history. As a young boy, I enjoyed reading books and visiting battlefields near my home like Fort Donelson

[1] Walter Lynn Bates, "Southern Unionists: A Socio-Economic Examination of the Third East Tennessee Volunteer Infantry Regiment U.S.A." *THQ* 50.4: 226.

and Shiloh. Studying my family history was a way for me to find my own connection to the war. I searched for a Confederate ancestor with the hope of becoming a member of the Sons of Confederate Veterans. But what I discovered was even more bewildering and fascinating: my great-great grandfather John Wesley Plunk, even though he was born and raised in McNairy County, Tennessee, was a *Union* cavalryman. He rode not with Nathan Bedford Forrest, but with Fielding Hurst.

Naturally my discovery led me to ask questions. What circumstances led to my great-great grandfather's decision and that of the other soldiers of the 6th Tennessee Cavalry to fight for the Union? How did their friends, neighbors, and family members who sided with the Confederacy react? What made Fielding Hurst, a man who was one of the largest slave owners in McNairy County, Tennessee, so vindictive against his fellow Southerners that he burned their homes and extorted money from them?

My first introduction to Fielding Hurst was a state historical marker in Bethel Springs, Tennessee. It described the Hurst family as "staunch Unionists in a predominantly Confederate area" who were led by Fielding Hurst "commanding the 6th Tennessee Cavalry, an irregular Union group which skirmished and scouted for various Federal commanders in the area." The regiment he organized and led was described by one Confederate soldier as "an ignorant posse of men led by vicious and unprincipled leaders" who were "the scourge and terror of the lower Eastern Counties of West Tennessee, and were as thoroughly detested and hated as any band of marauders who ever disgraced the name of soldiers."[2] Hatred for Hurst and his men has been passed down through generations of families in southwest Tennessee.

It is difficult to separate truth from fiction when chronicling the events that surround Hurst and his command. Their reputation among former Confederate soldiers and their families was understandably stained with the blood of relatives and friends. Unfortunately, there has been little written by members of the 6th Tennessee Cavalry that shed light on their experiences. As a result, much of what has been written and passed down about the regiment through post Civil War literature and oral histories has been

---

[2] William T. Alderson, ed. "The Civil War Reminiscences of John Johnston, 1861-1865." *Tennessee Historical Quarterly* 13:3 (September 1954): 272.

decidedly partisan in nature and accepted as truth by modern writers and historians.

This book is not only a regimental history but a biography of its organizer and leader as well, for Fielding Hurst and the Sixth Tennessee Cavalry are inseparable; one cannot be discussed without mentioning the other. It has a two-fold purpose. From a regimental standpoint, the book describes the activities of the 6th Tennessee during the war and offers insight into what motivated its soldiers to choose to fight with the Union armies that were invading their state. From an individual standpoint, it shares the experiences of Fielding Hurst, who was considered a traitor to his own people and to former Confederates and their descendants became the embodiment of the "homemade Yankee." My intention has been to write an objective account of Hurst and his command and describe the experiences of they and other Unionists in southwest Tennessee before, during, and after the war. My hope for the reader is to gain a better understanding of the man and the regiment and the arduous times in war-torn West Tennessee.

Kevin D. McCann
September 2007

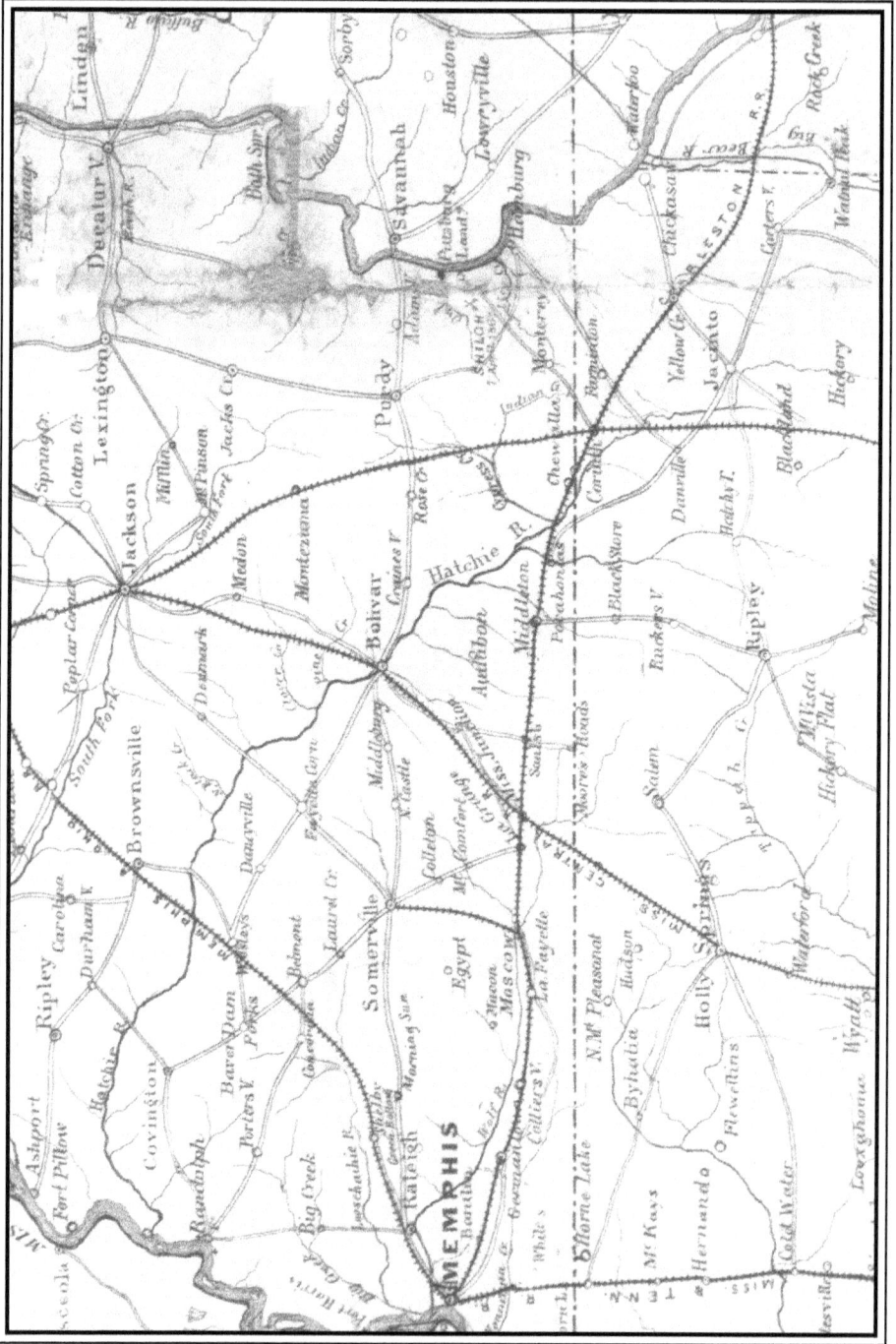

WEST TENNESSEE AND NORTH MISSISSIPPI
(O. LEDERLE, 1862, LIBRARY OF CONGRESS)

Despair for the children
who lie now in bed.
The widow, the aged
the soldier who bled.
For out of the "Nation"
comes a sickness and curse—
God save us all
from the demon called Hurst.

Like vandals of old
through our land they did ride.
With Hunger and Death
always close by their side.
Came Terror, his herald—
but the wailing comes first.
We know he is coming,
that demon called Hurst.

—Author unknown

HURST'S WURST

FORCED TO
CHOOSE SIDES
FEBRUARY – NOVEMBER 1861

C OURAGE WAS A REQUIREMENT for the men of Tennessee who went to the polls on June 8, 1861 with the intention of voting against secession. The pressure was intense to cast their ballots in favor of leaving the Union and joining other Southern states in the newly formed Confederate States of America. Tennessee Governor Isham Green Harris was unabashedly in favor of it and had already promised troops for its cause before the votes were even cast.[1] Influential newspaper editors and fiery stump speakers stoked the fires of separation and encouraged voters to openly display their ballots for all to see and applaud. The pro-union voters, casting theirs folded into the ballot boxes, were jeered and mocked as abolitionists and "Black Republicans" for their choice.[2]

It was the second statewide referendum on secession since the election of Abraham Lincoln as president seven months earlier. The first held on February 9 placed before the voters the choice to hold a convention on the subject and decide its members, choosing between pro-secession and pro-union candidates. The convention was rejected by 11,893 votes, yet two-

---

[1] Paul H. Bergeron, *Paths of the Past: Tennessee, 1770-1970* (Knoxville, TN: University of Tennessee Press, 1979): 57.
[2] Derek William Frisby, "'Homemade Yankees': West Tennessee Unionism in the Civil War Era." Doctoral dissertation, University of Alabama, 2004: 57-58, 60.

thirds of West Tennessee voters favored one but with pro-union candidates in control.[3]

In the wake of Lincoln's election, a convention of eight influential citizens of McNairy County—Richard Cross, Fielding Hurst, John H. Meeks, J.F. McKinney, A.A. Sanders, Stanford L. Warren, Dew M. Wisdom, and Congressman John V. Wright—met on December 3, 1860 to discuss its ramifications and future courses of action for their county and the state. While they were not pleased with the election of a sectional and divisive candidate such as Lincoln, its members reasoned that it was not sufficient cause for secession.[4]

The Unionists hoped for a peaceful resolution to the secession crisis. In the weeks before his inauguration, Lincoln maintained that the Federal coastal forts in Confederate hands would be retaken and custom duties would be collected from Southern ports. But the Unionist leaders of the upper South asked him to pursue a more passive policy. They proposed that the rebellious states be allowed to keep the forts and surrender those still in Federal control at Fort Sumter and Fort Pickens. With no reason for armed conflict, the seceded states would eventually return to the Union.[5]

Among the leaders of the pro-union effort in McNairy County was Lindsay Sanders, a fifty-four-year-old farmer from Stantonville. His brothers were divided by the secession debate: three opposed it and the three favored it. Indicative of his Christian beliefs and his unwavering devotion to his country was his last will and testament, which proclaimed:

> [N]o avowed infidel, atheist, deist, disunionist or secessionist shall ever be a beneficiary of our estate. And any American citizen so low and depraved in politics, so wanting in fidelity to our glorious Union as to desire a dissolution or a separation of our State from our sister States, is not only wholly unworthy of enjoying the good things afforded by the National Union but should be driven from the American soil.[6]

---

[3] Ibid: 44.

[4] Memphis *Appeal*, December 11, 1860. Charles L. Lufkin, "Divides Loyalties: Sectionalism in Civil War McNairy County, Tennessee." *THQ* 47.3 (Fall 1988): 170-171.

[5] Daniel W. Crofts, *Reluctant Confederates: Upper South Unionists in the Secession Crisis.* (Chapel Hill: University of North Carolina Press, 1989): 257.

[6] 1860 U.S. Census for McNairy County, Tennessee. *McNairy County History of Tennessee.* (Chicago and Nashville, TN: The Goodspeed Publishing Company, 1887): 3.

Sanders reported the state of affairs in his home county to U.S. Senator Andrew Johnson of Tennessee. "A great effort is being made to chain our noble Ten[nessee] to the Car of Secession," he wrote on February 5. "[T]he disunion orators and Editors are using every device in order to disgrace and shake down the best Patriots we have in the state." He believed two-thirds of his home county favored the Union but admitted that two-thirds of the citizens in the county seat of Purdy were secessionist.[7]

The tide of public sentiment in Tennessee shifted dramatically in the spring of 1861. While the attack on Fort Sumter by Confederate forces on April 12 was significant, it was not enough to tip the balance in favor of separation. This occurred three days later when President Lincoln called for 75,000 volunteers to suppress the rebellion. It created war fervor in the North and forced Southerners to choose sides.[8]

The proclamation helped secessionists convince voters that Lincoln intended to use military force to achieve his objectives. When Secretary of War Simon Cameron asked for two regiments of Tennessee militia, Governor Harris defiantly refused. "Tennessee will not furnish a single man for the purpose of Coercion [sic]," he answered, "but 50,000 if necessary for the defense of our rights and those of our Southern brothers."[9]

Many who had advocated patience and negotiation with the president now felt betrayed by him. Whether grudgingly or wholeheartedly, they were now compelled to join the secession movement they had fought against and defend their state against a Northern invasion. "However wrong the [secession] leaders may have acted," wrote John Houston Bills, a merchant from Bolivar, Tennessee, "no one will see the south coerced into submission."[10]

Harris called a special session of the state General Assembly on April 25. He endorsed legislation "formally declaring the independence of the State of Tennessee [from] the Federal Union, renouncing its authority, and reassum-

---

[7] Lindsay Sanders to Andrew Johnson, February 5, 1861. Andrew Johnson Papers (Library of Congress) on microfilm at TSLA.
[8] Crofts, *Reluctant Confederates*: 336.
[9] Isham G. Harris to Simon Cameron, April 15, 1861. Correspondence of Governor Isham G. Harris, 1861. TNGenWeb Project. <www.tngenweb.org/bios/h/18610429.html>
[10] Crofts, *Reluctant Confederates*: 337-338.

ing each and every function belonging to a separate sovereignty." He asked that preparations be made to enable it to join the Confederate states.[11] Lawmakers complied and a formal declaration of independence was signed on May 6. It still needed to be ratified through a voter referendum on June 8 to become official. In the meantime, the state formed a military alliance with the Confederacy.[12]

Secessionists used threats and intimidation to discourage Unionists from going to the polls and voting against it. In Memphis, colored ballots were printed to distinguish each vote, red for separation and blue for no separation. Pro-union advocates such as Congressman Emerson Etheridge who dared speak against secession were chased from the public forum. Newspapers sympathetic to their cause such as Issac Hawkins' *Carroll Patriot* in Huntingdon were shut down. Confederate soldiers made an intimidating presence at many polling places.[13]

Tennesseans voted overwhelmingly for separation 104,471 to 47,183. Unionist sentiment still existed primarily in East Tennessee, but it was evident in West Tennessee as well. While the majority voted 30,626 to 6,717 in favor of secession, the initiative failed in Carroll, Decatur, and Henderson counties and in Hardin and Wayne counties in southwest Middle Tennessee.[14]

The choice was made and Governor Harris mobilized the state's Provisional Army in earnest for service in the Confederacy. Rallies and barbeques were orchestrated to attract young men of military age and spirited orators appealed to them to enlist in the cause. But in the fall of 1861, patriotic appeals were replaced by a mandatory draft to satisfy the request for 30,000 additional troops made by Confederate General Albert Sidney Johnston. Lacking sufficient arms, the new recruits were supplied with weapons confiscated from private citizens through a newly enacted impressment law.[15]

---

[11] Isham G. Harris speech, April 25, 1861. Second Message of Governor Isham Harris to the Tennessee Assembly. <americancivilwar.com/documents/isham_harris_second.html>
[12] Robert E. Corlew, *Tennessee, A Short History* (Knoxville, TN: University of Tennessee Press, 1990): 293.
[13] Frisby, "Homemade Yankees": 57-58.
[14] Crofts, *Reluctant Confederates*: 342. Corlew, *Tennessee*: 295.
[15] Charles P. Roland, *Albert Sidney Johnston: Soldier of Three Republics*. (Austin: University of Texas Press, 1990): 275.

Life became increasingly difficult for those who held true to the Union in what was becoming enemy territory. Former friends and neighbors cursed them as "Lincolnites," "Black Republicans," abolitionists, cowards, and traitors and they were threatened for publicly expressing their Unionist sentiments. A sixty-one-year-old Hardin County farmer named William C. Hughes was threatened by a Confederate officer who "sent me word that if I did not stop my mouth about the war that he would have my d—d tongue cut out of my head, and his notice was in writing."[16] The Confederate Congress enacted legislation called the Alien Enemies Act that required allegiance to the new nation or face arrest, expulsion from the South, or even death. Unionists were arrested, brought to court, and charged with treason against the Confederacy.[17] "Union men was compelled to layout [sic], leave the County, go to prison, or enlist in the Rebel Army," recalled Fielding Hurst.[18]

Regardless, many loyalists in West Tennessee resisted the draft and refused to surrender their weapons. Some fled with their families north to Kentucky, Illinois, and Ohio; others hid in the woods and caves near their homes. Guns were "buried in the ground, hid in hollow logs, and under floors" to prevent being confiscated.[19] Braver men openly brandished their weapons and defiantly evaded the draft. In early January 1862, citizens in Weakley and Carroll counties held public demonstrations against it. Protesters in Henderson County would not even let the draft take place. The situation was especially volatile in McNairy County, where citizens armed themselves and troops had to be sent to restore order. As a result of the unrest, Governor Harris temporarily suspended the draft in those counties.[20]

The "Union feeling is very strong" in those counties, wrote a correspondent for the Chicago *Tribune*. All that was needed was "the appearance of the national troops to make a general uprising."[21] Some tried making their way to the Union armies at Paducah, Kentucky rather than wait for them to

---

16 William C. Hughes Southern Claims Commission No. 17798 <www.footnote.com>

17 Steve Cottrell, *Civil War in Tennessee*. (Gretna, LA: Pelican Publishing Company, 2001): 14.

18 Deposition of Fielding Hurst, May 2, 1873. Pitser M. Cheshier SCC No. 17782 <www.footnote.com>

19 "From Rebeldom." *New York Times*, January 3, 1862.

20 Ibid. Trenton *Standard*, January 10, 1862. TCWSB <www.tennessee.civilwarsourcebook.com> Fisby, "Homemade Yankees": 124.

21 Chicago *Tribune*, December 11, 1861.

appear. In November 1861, Nathan McDonald Kemp, deputy sheriff of Hardin County, and William C. Hughes traveled to Paducah 160 miles on foot with nightfall as their cover to learn "our prospect for deliverance." They met with Brigadier General Eleazer A. Paine, the post commander, who told them to "tell the Union men to stand their ground and that the gun boats would soon be up the river and all would be well."[22]

When Kemp and Hughes returned home, local Confederate authorities learned the nature of their trip and intended to arrest them. They decided to go back to Paducah on December 11 with a group of forty loyal neighbors. But Confederate cavalry and a civilian posse pursued them and apprehended about half of them four miles north of Decaturville. "[W]e scatered [sic] on to different roads and in to the woods," recalled Kemp, but "the whole country was alive with rebel cav[alry] and armed citizens laying in wait for us."[23]

Some men like twenty-four-year-old Pitser M. Cheshier were forced into the Confederate army against their will. He was a farmer at McNairy Station known in his neighborhood for his Union sentiments. But his father-in-law, "a man of wealth and great influence," sided with the Confederacy and threatened to have him arrested if he did not enlist in the Confederate army. "[T]he Union men was then being arrested, and put in guard Houses, and Jailes, [sic] and abused in other ways," he recalled. "So I volunteered in the Confederate army but not with my own concent [sic] for I was not for the Rebels." Years later when he explained why he had been a Confederate solder, he wrote: "I was not Conscripted in to the Servis [sic]; I was Scared into it."[24]

Others joined to escape harassment from their rebel neighbors, then deserted when they had the opportunity and enlisted in the Union army. Jackson J. King intended to make his way north with his brother John C. King and friend James W. Clifton to join the Union army in the fall of 1861. But he got into an argument with a secessionist named M.V. Lacefield at a gathering of the local militia when he vowed that he "would never fight for the Southern Confederacy." Lacefield said he would kill him for being "a

[22] Depositions of Nathan McDonald Kemp and William C. Hughes in William C. Hughes SCC No. 17798 <www.footnote.com> "Life of N.M.D. Kemp." Clifton (TN) Mirror, June 16, 1905. Kemp Family Chronicles website. August 12, 2007. <www.kempchronicles.com/doc.hmtl>
[23] Kemp Deposition, Hughes SCC 17798. Hughes identified the cavalry as "Taylor's Company." Hughes Deposition, Ibid.
[24] Deposition of Pitser M. Cheshier, May 2, 1873. Cheshier SCC 17782.

d—d Tory" and stabbed him ten times, but it was King and his brother who were arrested by Confederate authorities.[25]

King's father sought the advice of Unionist friends. They suggested it might be best for his sons to join the Confederate army and avoid prosecution for the altercation and further retaliation from Lacefield and his friends. They enlisted, but Jackson spent most of his time in military hospitals for illness and "never had a gun in my hand." He was taken prisoner after the battle at Island No. 10 on the Mississippi River. He tried to renounce the Confederacy and join the Union army, but he was not allowed to do so. Finally he deserted in July 1863 and made his way back to McNairy County where he promptly enlisted in Company G of the 6th Tennessee Cavalry.[26]

---

[25] Deposition of Jackson J. King, February 23, 1878. Jackson J. King SCC No. 17806 <www.footnote.com>

[26] Ibid. Deposition of James W. Clifton, February 23, 1878. King SCC 17806.

A NATION
ONTO HIMSELF
NOVEMBER 1861 – AUGUST 1862

FIELDING JACKSON HURST HAD EVERYTHING TO LOSE taking a stand for the Union. At fifty-one-years old, he was a prosperous and wealthy farmer, merchant, and lawyer in McNairy County. He was also one of its largest landowners and slave owners and a charter member of the Masonic lodge in Purdy, Tennessee.

Hurst was also a man of strong, unwavering convictions. One of his captors when he was arrested for speaking out against secession determined he was "a very intelligent, shrewd fellow" in the short time he was with him. John A. Pitts, who represented Hurst as his attorney on several occasions, described him as "a very sensible man though full of prejudice, fractious and litigious, utterly devoid of any sense of humor, serious on all subjects." Another acquaintance believed if "his enemies had let him alone, that his course would have been far different." But this was a time when men had to choose sides and Fielding Hurst followed his convictions.[1]

He was born in 1810 on the farm of his parents Elijah and Margaret Breeding Hurst on Big Barren Creek in Claiborne County, situated in the mountains of northeastern Tennessee. He was the second of six sons and three daughters. At about nineteen years old, he married Melocky

---

[1] Samuel Mills Meek to wife, December 4, 1861, Colleen Holland personal collection. John A. Pitts, *Personal and Professional Reminiscences of an Old Lawyer.* (Kingsport, TN: Southern Publishers, 1930): 184. Jeff Walker, "Early History of McNairy County." *McNairy County Independent*, November 23, 1923.

Huddleston at her parents' home in Claiborne County on March 4, 1830.[2] Her uncle Thomas Huddleston had left Claiborne County and settled west of the Tennessee River in McNairy County. Hurst and his bride joined him in December 1833. Seven years later, Hurst's parents and siblings as well as three of Melocky's brothers and their families also settled there.[3]

Hurst served two terms as county surveyor, giving him extensive knowledge of available land. He and his five brothers acquired a large amount of acreage in northwest McNairy County (and present-day Chester County) that covered an estimated twenty-one square miles[4]. Because they owned the land, they also controlled the roads within its borders. During the war, this territory became known as the "Hurst Nation." It acquired a reputation—often undeserved—for robbery and murder of unwanted visitors.[5]

The Hursts and their related families were a close-knit clan that lived in close proximity to one another. Despite being the second oldest brother next to Arthur Hurst, Fielding was considered the family leader especially after the death of his father Elijah Hurst in 1857. When he made the decision to stand with the Union, most of them followed suit. The exception was a younger brother, David Hurst, who felt he should be compensated for the emancipation of his slaves. He sided with the Confederacy instead.[6]

As one of the largest slaveowners in the county, Fielding Hurst should have been among the secessionist leaders. It only seemed natural that he would favor the Confederacy, preserving his way of life instead of siding with the Union and becoming a pariah in his own community. One reason for his decision may have been his East Tennessee roots. His personality as a child and a young man was forged in the mountains where stories of the brave men that fought the Tories at the Battle of King's Mountain during the American Revolution nurtured in its people an innate devotion for their

---

[2] Virginia Branch, *The Hurst Nation: A Family History* (Paragould: Virginia Branch, 1987): 6-7. Melocky Hurst Widow Pension Application.

[3] 1830 and 1840 U.S. Censuses for McNairy County, Tennessee.

[4] George Lapides, "Story of Col. Hurst, the Fearless Yankee." Memphis *Press-Scimitar*, February 19, 1963. The Hurst Nation stretched from south of Woodville to north of Montezuma and included Masseyville.

[5] Gary R. Blankenship, "Colonel Fielding Hurst and the Hurst Nation." *West Tennessee Historical Society Papers* (October 1980): 72. Branch, *The Hurst Nation*: 6-7. Franklin Mitchell, *The Hurst Nation and Its People* (Selmer, TN: G & P Printing Services, 2003): 89.

[6] Blankenship, "Hurst": 74

country.[7] No doubt he heard stories of the part his grandfather "Mill Creek" John Hurst played in the struggle as a Virginia Militiaman, stories that would have made an impression on his moral conscience.[8] He was about fifty-one years old in 1861, more socially and politically conservative and less impetuous than the typically younger and more zealous men who espoused secession.[9]

Hurst was loyal to the Union, but he was no abolitionist. When the war began, he owned as many as twenty-three slaves; two of them, Lloyd and Sam, accompanied him as servants during the conflict. "They treated me good," recalled one former slave, Ab Hurst, about the Hurst and Walker families who owned him. "I picked cotton, made cross-ties and cut wood, but never did have to work too hard."[10] As the war progressed, however, Hurst decided to give them their freedom when it was over. But he never had the chance: they were stolen from his farm in February 1864 and sold by Confederate soldiers "raising funds to fight for the rebellion."[11]

Hurst endured persecution from his secessionist neighbors just as other Unionists experienced throughout West Tennessee. His prominence in the community no doubt made it even more difficult. Between June 1861 and February 1862, he had been arrested and imprisoned at least three times. He shared his experiences with Charles Carleton Coffin, a war correspondent for the Boston *Daily Journal* who traveled with the Army of the Tennessee in the spring of 1862.[12]

According to Coffin, Hurst initially kept his pro-union sentiments to himself, but the more ardent secessionists in Purdy suspected his true beliefs. It was not long after the referendum passed that he received a visit from members of a local vigilance committee. Despite their best efforts that summer, he refused to be intimidated but did not give them cause to incriminate him. Hurst claimed in September 1861 that the group arrested him on charges of being an abolitionist and a spy and threw him in jail, his

---

[7] William C. Harris, *With Charity For All: Lincoln and the Restoration of the Union* (Lexington, KY: University Press of Kentucky, 1999): 28.

[8] Branch, *The Hurst Nation*: 4.

[9] Lufkin, "Divided Loyalties" *THQ* 47.3: 176-177.

[10] Dale Blair, "Heard Roar of Shiloh Guns as Boy Slave, Negro Claims." Memphis *Commercial-Appeal*, September 3, 1963.

[11] Hurst to W.H. Morgan, September 15, 1864. Hurst Military Records.

[12] Charles Carleton Coffin, *My Days and Nights on the Battlefield* (Boston, MA: Dana Estes and Company, 1887): 270. Memphis *Bulletin*, March 26, 1862. *New York Times*, November 9, 1862.

cell being "a cage, so small that he could not lie down."[13] He was incarcerated for two days before being sent to Nashville for trial. Some of his neighbors "who owed him a grudge…invented lies [and] swore that Hurst was in communication with the Yankees, and gave them information of all the movements of the Rebels."[14] He was found guilty of being a spy and sentenced to death, but he was saved by the intervention of less hardened secessionists, supposedly with the hangman's noose already around his neck. It was decided instead that he report his whereabouts periodically to local authorities and he was released.[15]

But a speech given by Hurst at Purdy proved to be the last straw.[16] On November 27, 1861, a company of Confederate soldiers dispatched from Corinth, Mississippi arrested him and four or five other Union sympathizers in McNairy County. A sixth man (believed to be Lindsey Sanders) escaped when the soldiers surrounded his home and a gunfight ensued. Three of his sons weren't as fortunate.[17] The prisoners were taken to Corinth, where the Confederate marshal for Middle Tennessee took custody of them and sent them to Nashville for trial. Captain Samuel Mills Meek Jr. with Company H of the 35th Mississippi Infantry was among the men who escorted them to the train station. He wrote:

> As we marched them through the streets [to the railroad station],
> we were surrounded by a dense crowd of excited, curious people,
> all anxious to get a sight of the 'infernal Lincanites [*sic*]' as they
> called them. It was truly an awful sight to see men, born upon
> Southern soil, compelled to be marched like felons through the

---

[13] Coffin, *Days and Nights*: 272.

[14] Ibid: 272-273.

[15] Ibid: 273.

[16] Fielding Hurst Deposition. William C. Hughes Southern Claims Commission No. 17798. The exact date of Hurst's speech is not known. He wrote: "[I] lay in prison with [William C. Hughes] at Nashville, Tennessee, where I had been lodged on account of a Union Speech I made in this town [Purdy] on the first Monday of [*blank*] 1861." Ibid. J.W. Purviance, an attorney and newspaper publisher in McNairy County, recalled: "The treatment [Hurst] received from some of the citizens of Purdy, who had him arrested, put in chains and taken to Nashville, and for six weeks laid on the cold stone floors of the penitentiary, all because he had made a speech in Purdy opposing secession was enough to cause him…to vent some of his vengeance on those who drove him to the fighting lines." W.V. Barry, "A Long Time Ago." *McNairy County Independent*, 18 January 1924.

[17] The 1860 Census for McNairy County shows Lindsey Saunders' three oldest sons as being Byron L. (age 26), Lindsey (age 24), and Stanford L. (age 22). After the war, Hurst wrote: "I was forced to leave my house, and otherwise abused, had my family abused, and property destroyed." Hurst deposition, Cheshier SCC 17782.

streets of a town not 20 miles from their residence, charged with
Treason to their State and their Section.[18]

At Nashville they were tried before West Hughes Humphreys, judge for
the Confederate District Court of Tennessee, and charged with inciting a
"Union insurrectionary assemblage." They were allowed to post bail and
return to McNairy County to gather evidence for their defense. The hearing
was held on December 16. Two men were released when they took an oath
of allegiance to the Confederacy and another was released for "his good
behavior." Fielding Hurst and one of the Sanders brothers refused to
comply and were imprisoned. "This attempt of the Unionists of McNairy
county [*sic*] to make a call by the [Confederate] Government for troops a
pretext for the execution of their treasonable scheme, has proven a miser-
able abortion," opined the Nashville *Union and American* writer who covered
the trial. "It died out after their leader, Hurst, a lawyer of some force of
character, was taken from them."[19]

Hurst was imprisoned for thirty-seven days before he was released on
January 27, 1862. Disloyal citizens were required to take an oath of allegiance to the Confederacy, but he was not made to do so. "I think the oath
of allegiance was administered to some of the prisoners," recalled Hurst,
"but Judge Humphrey[s] sayed [*sic*] that he did not care whether I [had]
taken the oath of allegiance or not for he knew I would not keep it if I did
take it."[20]According to one account, Humphreys sentenced Hurst to be
hanged on April 7, 1862. But the intervention of a friend with ties to the
Confederate government in Richmond enabled him to be paroled in January
and escape the death sentence.[21]

Hurst returned to his home in Purdy and found his secessionist
neighbors had ransacked his farm. His livestock and horses had been stolen
and his family's food, including several thousand pounds of bacon, had been

---

[18] Samuel Mills Meek to wife, December 4, 1861, Colleen Holland personal collection. "I conversed
with them freely," Meeks wrote, "and they some what excited my sympathies, as they talked of their
families at home, but if they are guilty, they do not deserve the communication of any human beings."
Ibid. Meeks' company and regiment were verified on the National Park Service Civil War Soldiers and
Sailors online database <www.itd.nps.gov/cwss/index.html>
[19] Nashville *Union and American*, December 17, 1861.
[20] Nashville *Union and American*, December 17, 1861. *Nashville Republican Banner*, December 17, 1861.
Memphis *Bulletin*, March 26, 1865. This article claimed he served at the state penitentiary in Nashville,
but there is no record of his imprisonment there. Charles Sherrill, *Tennessee Convicts: Early Records of the
State Penitentiary Volume 2, 1850-1870*. Hurst Deposition for Hughes Claim.
[21] Memphis *Bulletin*, March 26, 1865.

plundered.[22] Ten days later, he was arrested once again and sent to Columbus, Kentucky, where Confederate General Leonidas Polk intended to impose the death sentence after all. Escorted back to McNairy County by a military guard sent to uncover evidence of his Unionist activities, Hurst escaped and hid for a week in the swampy bottoms of the Tennessee River. He was rescued along with fourteen other refugees by the wooden gunboat USS *Tyler*. He even participated in a battle with it and the USS *Lexington* against a rebel battery at Pittsburg Landing on March 1.[23]

Coffin described another daring escape by Hurst. Learning that men were coming to his home to arrest him, he told one of his young slaves to saddle and harness his horse and take it behind a local drugstore. Hurst left through the back door, brazenly walked down the street for onlookers who awaited his arrest to see, and entered the drugstore. He summoned the druggist to the back of the store and drew a pistol to his head. "If you make any noise, I will blow your brains out!" threatened Hurst. He feinted that he had four friends ready to kill the druggist if he gave him away. Hurst opened the back door where the young boy and his horse waited in the alley. He climbed on and made his escape.[24]

***

The fall of Fort Henry on the Tennessee River and Fort Donelson on the Cumberland River in February 1862 allowed the invading Federal armies to penetrate the Confederacy. Governor Harris and the Tennessee government abandoned the state capital at Nashville and fled to Memphis. President Lincoln appointed U.S. Senator Andrew Johnson of Tennessee as military governor of the state with the rank of brigadier general.[25]

---

[22] Fielding Hurst to William H. Morgan, September 15, 1864. Fielding Hurst Military Records.
[23] Memphis *Bulletin*, March 26, 1865. One contemporary account claimed he was imprisoned a third time as well. *New York Times*, November 9, 1862.
[24] Coffin, *Days and Nights*: 273-274. Slightly different versions are given in Frazer Kirkland, *The Pictorial Book of Anecdotes and Incidents of the War of the Rebellion* (Hartford, CT: Hartford Publishing Company, 1867): 98-99 and A Member of the G.A.R., *The Picket Line and Camp Fire Stories; A Collection of War Anecdotes* (New York, Hurst & Co., n.d.): 37-41. Coffin claimed it was after this escape that Hurst made his way to the Union armies near Pittsburgh Landing. This claim contradicts the account given in the Memphis *Bulletin* on March 26, 1865.
[25] Richard Nelson Current, *Lincoln's Loyalists: Union Soldiers from the Confederacy* (New York: Oxford University Press, 1992): 43.

As Federal gunboats made their way up the Tennessee River, the loyal citizens of West Tennessee enthusiastically welcomed them. Lieutenant William Gwin of the USS *Tyler* reported that Unionist sentiment was strong in the counties along the river. He encouraged his superior officers to station a brigade or cavalry unit at the river port town of Savannah, where their presence would embolden loyalists in the region "without fear of being mobbed" by the secessionists that harassed them. "I have warned the inhabitants of the different towns of the river that I would hold secessionists and their property responsible for any outrages committed on Unionists in their community," he wrote. Many men demonstrated their loyalty by enlisting in the Northern armies.[26]

Fielding Hurst organized a group of loyalists and offered their services as scouts and spies to the Union armies that were making their way through West Tennessee in March 1862. They were dressed in makeshift, homemade uniforms; Hurst himself wore "a tall silk hat, a long coat with brass buttons, baggy jeans pantaloons, and an old sword." The group was attached to Major General Lew Wallace's command at Crump Landing and operated in the vicinity of Pittsburg Landing and eastern McNairy County.[27] Hurst supposedly returned to Purdy with Wallace's command, went to the jail, and locked up the jailer—the same one who had taken pleasure in Hurst's arrest a few months earlier—in the same small cage that Hurst had been confined. When the jailer initially hesitated to go inside, Hurst reportedly took a bayoneted rifle from one of the Union soldiers and exclaimed, "Step in, I say, or I'll let daylight through you!"[28]

Brigadier General Grenville M. Dodge recognized the potential of Hurst's scouts as valuable sources of information in the West Tennessee

---

[26] *O.R.I*, 7:421. Frisby, "Homemade Yankees": 126.

[27] Jacob R. Perkins, *Trails, Rails, and War: The Life of General G.M. Dodge* (Indianapolis, IN: The Bobbs-Merrill Company, 1929): 109-110. A telegraph between members of the Army of the Tennessee dated May 5, 1862 indicated that Hurst was "in Genl Wallaces [*sic*] camp." Elijah Hurst file. Union Provost Marshal's File of Papers Relating to Individual Citizens. Microfilm No. 138 at TSLA.

[28] Coffin, *Days and Nights*: 273-274. According to Coffin, Hurst left the jailer locked up for two days before discovering he had lost the key. Ibid. The version of this story contained in *The Picket Line and Camp Fire Stories*: 40-41 claimed it was a secessionist neighbor arrested and not the jailer that was thrown in jail.

backwoods. Unlike the invading Northerners, they were residents of the area and familiar with the roads, the terrain, and the people. Dodge's biographer noted that Hurst's command could distinguish "a company, regiment, brigade or division by the space occupied in the field or along the road." The Federal commander also used them as spies working behind enemy lines. They relayed information back to him through women allowed to go back and forth visiting relatives.[29]

Hurst and his men tended to stray from the main army, a trait that continued over the course of the war. "I noticed when I went on an expedition through their country," recalled Dodge after the war, "that in the afternoon Colonel Hurst's regiment would grow less and less until by night he had hardly a company left; then they would gather in the morning and catch us on the march, for they seemed to know our position intuitively, and by noon he would have a full regiment present." He added, "I often told Colonel Hurst that if I got into a fight I hoped it would be about noon so I could have the services of his regiment."[30]

Hurst's command became a nuisance to local Confederate forces, harassing pickets and cutting telegraph lines in the area. They were skilled at evading capture through their knowledge "of every hog-path in the country" to escape. The commanding officer at Bethel Station was forced to assign more soldiers to picket duty because of the disturbances. "I find the country troublesome to picket, as there are innumerable by-ways and paths leading in every direction," lamented Confederate Brigadier General Samuel B. Maxey, "and a man like Hurst, who is piloting the Federals about, or any of his gang, can take a body almost anywhere unobserved if they once learn the points picketed."[31]

They were also successful at disabling tracks on the Mobile and Ohio Railroad and hindering rebel supply trains from reaching Corinth, Mississippi. Colonel A.J. Lindsay of the 1st Mississippi Cavalry reported on May 5 that Hurst skirmished with the pickets near Purdy and intended to break the railroad line. "By going through the woods with small parties," he wrote,

---

[29] Perkins, *Trails, Rails, and War.* 110.

[30] Ibid.

[31] O.R. I, 10, part 2: 456. Another example of Hurst harassing Confederate pickets may be found in Marcus J. Wright, *Diary from April 23, 1861 to February 26, 1863*. Civil War Collection, Box 7, Folder 11:5 at TSLA.

"they can tap the railroad anywhere they choose out of reach of my pickets."[32]

But Hurst wanted a more active role in the war than simply being a scout. He and James W. Tarkington[33] of Henderson County recruited enough loyal men to form five companies and on July 23, they asked Military Governor Andrew Johnson for commissions to form a new cavalry regiment. Tarkington would serve as colonel and Hurst as lieutenant colonel. They were anxious to receive their commissions; the Rebels were "getting very bold" in the region, they wrote, "some of whom have taken the oath [of allegiance]." [34]

Their plea was reinforced two days later by Major General Ulysses S. Grant, who described Hurst as "a refugee from his home [who] has acted as guide & scout for the army." But Johnson, preoccupied with liberating his home region of East Tennessee from Confederate control, would not authorize commissions to raise Union regiments for West Tennessee. Exasperated with the governor's resistance, Hurst traveled to Nashville and asked Johnson for the commission in person. Tarkington's role had evidently diminished and Hurst received a commission as colonel of the 1st West Tennessee Cavalry on August 12, 1862.[35]

---

[32] O.R. I, 10, part 2: 493.

[33] James White Tarkington (1806-1868) was listed in the 1860 U.S. Census for Henderson County as a 53-year-old farmer. 1860 U.S. Census, Series M653, Roll1256: 292. Heritage Quest Online. He became sheriff of Dyer County, Tennessee in 1865. Sarah Armistead. "Re: J.W. Tarkington Henderson Co. TN 1860." Online posting. November 7, 2006. Tarkington Family Genealogy Forum. <genforum.genealogy.com/tarkington/messages/73.html>

[34] John Simon, ed. *The Papers of Ulysses S. Grant*. (Carbondale, IL: Southern Illinois University Press, 1973) 5:236

[35] Ibid. Johnson wrote Major General John A. McClernand: "I have commissioned Fielding Hurst Colonel of [the] 1st West Tenn Cavalry...I hope you will give Colonel Hurst all the aid and instructions you can in obtaining subsistence & supplies." Johnson to McClernand, 12 August 1862. Leroy P. Graf and Ralph W. Haskins, eds. *The Papers of Andrew Johnson, Vol. 5: 1861-1862*. (Knoxville, TN: University of Tennessee Press, 1979) 5:611.

ONE COUNTRY, ONE LANGUAGE, ONE FLAG

AUGUST – DECEMBER 1862

T HE NEWLY COMMISSIONED COLONEL FIELDING HURST returned from Nashville on August 20 and began vigorously recruiting volunteers for his new regiment. He traveled through five counties in a little over a month and enlisted over 1,200 men. As he did so, his Unionist allies began organizing men from McNairy County one half mile south of Bethel Station. The first company, designated as Company A, was created on August 11 and Robert M. Thompson was elected captain.[1]

In the weeks that followed, five additional companies were organized: Company B on August 25, with Harry Hodges as captain; Company C on September 11, Nathan McDonald Kemp captain; Company D on September 12, Levi Hurst captain; Company E on September 18, Elijah Roberts captain; and Company F on September 21, Daniel I. Dickerson captain. They even adopted a regimental motto: "I give my head and my heart to God and our country—one country, one language, one flag."[2]

Like Hurst, most of the enlisted men had little or no prior military experience; before the war, they had been lawyers, merchants, schoolteachers, ministers, and farmers.[3] They enlisted in the regiment for a variety of reasons. The most common was genuine patriotism. Many wanted the

---

[1] TITCW 1:333. "History of the Sixth Tenn. Cavalry" in *McNairy County Independent*, 11 September 1903.
[2] "History of the Sixth Tenn. Cavalry" in *McNairy County Independent*, 11 September 1903.
[3] Memphis *Bulletin*, March 26, 1865. Hurst to Johnson, March 11, 1863. RLB.

Union to be preserved and not broken apart. Their grandfathers had fought and some had died for American independence almost 90 years earlier.[4] Others simply could not turn their backs on their country. "I always adhered to the Union and I still do," wrote recruiter William C. Hughes after the war. "I never was one of those men that thought more of my state than the whole government."[5] Before he died, Sergeant James Thomas Wolverton of Company G purchased an American flag to be placed on his coffin. "He loved the flag so much that patriotism was almost a religion with him," recalled his son.[6]

Not all recruits enlisted of their own free will. Four Kirk cousins from Tishomingo County, Mississippi who were visiting relatives in McNairy County went to Pocahontas, where members of the regiment "invited" the cousins to join their unit.[7] Nineteen-year-old Stephen W. Fish of Hardeman County joined Company A on January 6, 1864 rather than let its soldiers take his favorite horse from him.[8]

One Arkansas Unionist's description of the fortitude of his fellow Unionists—"men of uncommon nerve" he called them—and the sacrifices they made during the war could also be applied to the men of the 1st West Tennessee:

> Few men are possessed of moral courage enough to publicly commit themselves to a cause surrounded with the dangers of Unionism in Rebeldom! It costs our northern friends nothing, but rather they are well paid for their loyalty. Not so with the loyal citizen who may at this unfortunate time have his home in the "sunny south," it costs him his all for the time being, and [he] is often but little rewarded for it.[9]

The 1st West Tennessee Cavalry, composed of six companies, was assigned to the Union post at Bethel Station commanded by Colonel Isham Nicholas Haynie of the 48th Illinois Cavalry. During this time, a detachment led by Colonel Hurst marched to Corinth, Mississippi under the command

[4] Current, *Lincoln's Loyalists*: 139, 145-146.
[5] William C. Hughes SCC No. 17798.
[6] Horace May Wolverton, "James Thomas Wolverton." (Unpublished article courtesy of Susie Summers.)
[7] Reflections Committee, *Reflections*: 498.
[8] Bill Wagoner, *Shiloh Remembered: A Collection of Bill Wagoner's Wagon Spokes* (Adamsville, TN: Banner Publishing Company, 1987): 8.
[9] Current, *Lincoln's Loyalists*: 146-147.

of Colonel Michael Kelly Lawler on October 3. They were too late to participate in the battle there, but they joined the pursuit of Confederate General Earl Van Dorn from Corinth to Ripley, Mississippi.[10]

Hurst continued recruiting loyal men from the surrounding area until ordered to stop ten days after his regiment's arrival on post. Haynie also sent 300 of Hurst's recruits to join Colonel Isaac R. Hawkins' 2nd West Tennessee Cavalry at Trenton, promising that they could enlist for twelve months under Hawkins rather than three years under Hurst. Other recruits left camp after "seeing the Ill treatment [that] Tennesseans Received at the hands of the authorities from southern Ill[inois]" and refused to serve.[11]

The interference and deceitfulness led Hurst to relocate his regiment away from the control of Haynie, whom he disdainfully described as "a little drunken Irishman."[12] Without authorization, he moved it fifty miles south to Ripley, Mississippi and obtained permission from Colonel John K. Mizner to resume his recruitment activities at nearby Clayton Station. Major General Ulysses S. Grant asked District of Corinth commander Major General William S. Rosecrans why Hurst was not following orders from his commander in the District of Jackson, Major General Stephen A. Hurlbut. Rosecrans replied that Hurst asked Mizner to let him to relocate to Clayton Station to "better organize his Reg[imen]t there." Mizner approved the move but denied ordering Hurst there.[13]

Hurlbut believed Colonel Hurst's insubordination was sufficient for a court-martial yet he was uncertain if Hurst was even a commissioned officer. "I have no evidence that he is," he wrote Major John A. Rawlins of Grant's staff, "[and] it may make a question if he be not." Rawlins confirmed that he had indeed been commissioned "and will be regarded and treated as in the service, and subject to the same regulations."[14]

Hurst and his men were valuable assets as scouts and spies in a region unfamiliar to the Union occupation forces, but their unofficial activities and close proximity to their homes and families proved to be detrimental.

---

10 TITCW 1:333.

11 Hurst to Johnson, March 11, 1863 in RLB. On 2 September 1862, Haynie wrote Brig. Gen. John A. Logan, post commander at Jackson, TN: "Col. Hurst requests to be sent up to Jackson under arrest[.] [C]an I do so[?] I think it Best[.]" It is not certain what circumstance led to this curious message, but it may be evidence of Hurst's dissatisfaction with Haynie. Hurst Military Records.

12 Ibid.

13 Simon, *Papers of Grant* 5:196fn.

14 Ibid.

Colonel William R. Morrison, who was stationed at Bethel Station with the 1st West Tennessee, believed the regiment was "made up of deserters from [the] Rebels & other bad men." It was "impossible to control them" as some went about the countryside waging private battles against their secessionist neighbors. Most of the regiment's horses had been stolen from citizens but they had been made to return them to their owners. "[I]n most cases, people dont [*sic*] complain [because they are] restrained by fear," Morrison wrote. He thought it best that the regiment be sent elsewhere.[15]

Major General Grant also became irritated at the 1st West Tennessee Cavalry's eagerness to seize horses from civilians. He wrote the new post commander at Bethel Station, Colonel John A. Logan, on October 25:

> Complaints are constantly coming to me of depredations committed by Hurst's men on Citizens [*sic*] through the country. They go about the country taking horses wherever they find them. They must desist from this practice or I will disband the whole concern. When horses are claimed by citizens, and there is no satisfactory reason why they should be taken, have them returned.[16]

That same day, the 1st West Tennessee was sent further away from their homes and families. They were ordered to report to Major General James P. McPherson at the Union post in Bolivar, Tennessee some 30 miles west of Bethel Station. A Chicago newspaper correspondent noted with curiosity their arrival on October 28:

> On Tuesday last our soldiery were surprised at the arrival among us of a Tennessee cavalry regiment, which encamped near the town. They looked very much like a lot of "secesh" [*sic*] as they made their "grand *entrée*," mounted as they were on a variety of horses, black, brown, white and "yaller," fat and lean, sound and spavined. Some of them had saddles, others not. Some of the chargers were curbed by the bit, others guided by rope halters. Their arms were in keeping with the rest. Some of the men carried at "right shoulder shift" a huge musket with the bayonet attached; others had a double-barreled shot-gun lengthwise across

---

15 Ibid
16 Ibid:195-196.

the saddle; others the squirrel rifle; and none of them the sabre [*sic*].[17]

Upon assuming command of the post a week later, Brigadier General Mason Brayman[18] noted the 1st West Tennessee Cavalry among his stationed forces, 600 men strong. But the regiment lacked sufficient weapons, equipment, and military training, so the new commander utilized them for little more than scouting and picket duty. Brayman was sympathetic to his plight: Hurst "has suffered Embarrassment because of the deficiency" and needed "Experienced officers to aid in discipline and drilling his men," he wrote. The regiment had not even been mustered into service, a necessity that was finally performed on November 15.[19]

To help Colonel Hurst train his men, Brayman recommended that Captain Daniel M. Emerson of his command be transferred to the 1st West Tennessee. Hurst welcomed Emerson's assistance and requested a commission to promote Emerson as major of the 2nd Battalion of his regiment. "He is an officer well acquainted with Discipline and drill," he wrote Andrew Johnson on December 4. "[He is] well educated, of good habits and high character, and will be of great Service to me in bringing my regiment at once into the field." The commission was approved but within six months, Major Emerson asked to be relieved of his command. Being "a northern man" appointed "against the wishes of the officers & men" of his command, he felt that he would be of greater service to the Union cause elsewhere "in a more advantageous position." His resignation was approved in July 1863.[20]

---

[17] "A Loyal Tennessee Cavalry Regiment." *New York Times*, November 9, 1862. The article referred to its commander as "Phelon Hurst," whose multiple imprisonments made him "just as much a martyr as Parson [William G.] Brownlow." Ibid.

[18] Mason Brayman (1813-1895) was a newspaper editor and lawyer in New York, Michigan and Illinois before receiving a commission as a major in the 19th Illinois Infantry at the start of the war. He was elevated to brigadier general retroactive to September 24, 1862. A veteran of the battles of Belmont, Fort Donelson, and Shiloh, Brayman assumed command of the Union post at Bolivar, Tennessee on November 3, 1862. He resumed his journalism career after the war and became governor of the Idaho territory in 1876. GIB: 44.

[19] Mason Brayman to Andrew Johnson, December 4, 1862 in Andrew Johnson Papers on microfilm, Series 1, Reel 6 at TSLA. Field and Staff Muster Rolls for the 6th Tennessee Cavalry (U.S.) photocopies courtesy of Jack Darrel Wood at JMCL.

[20] Hurst to Johnson, December 4, 1862 in Andrew Johnson Papers on microfilm, Series 1, Reel 6 at TSLA. Daniel M. Emerson to John A. Rawlins, June 28, 1863 in Daniel M. Emerson Military Records on microfilm at TSLA.

On December 10, 1862, Hurst reported to Lieutenant Colonel John A. Rawlins, Assistant Adjutant General of the Department of the Tennessee, that he had six companies and one hundred recruits who refused to be mustered into service "untill [*sic*] they see some prospect of being Armed and Equipped." It had been four months since the regiment was initially organized yet it had received no arms or equipment until the first of December. What it had been given was not sufficient for each man in the regiment. "I cannot recruit unless my men can have some Encouragement in the way of an outfit," wrote Hurst. He asked for 500 additional sharps carbines, 800 colt revolvers, 400 sabers, and 700 saddles and bridles. "[G]ive us these things & we will do the fighting," he assured Rawlins.[21]

Brigadier General Brayman was ordered to send all his available forces to Jackson, Tennessee on December 18. Eighty-three dismounted soldiers of the 1st West Tennessee under Major Emerson along with portions of the 43rd and 61st Illinois Infantry and the Springfield Artillery arrived by train that same day. The threat was Confederate cavalry leader Nathan Bedford Forrest, one that the regiment would become familiar with over the course of the war. Forrest was within five miles of Jackson with about 2,500 men (overestimated by Federal forces as between 3,000 and 20,000).[22]

While the rest of Brayman's command remained to defend Jackson, the 1st West Tennessee under Captain Robert M. Thompson of Company A was ordered to pursue the enemy cavalry at Trenton. On their way, the detachment skirmished the next day with Confederates forces along the Mobile and Ohio Railroad between Jackson and Humboldt. The clash led to the recapture of Humboldt by the Union army with no casualties suffered. Once reinforcements arrived, they returned to the post at Bolivar.[23]

A second detachment of the 1st West Tennessee operated in the vicinity of Trenton during this period. On December 27, it was ordered to Humboldt but engaged in "a heavy skirmish" with portions of Forrest's

---

[21] Hurst to Rawlins, December 10, 1862 in RLB.
[22] U.S. War Department. *The War of the Rebellion: A Compilation of the Official Records of the Union and Confederate Armies* (Washington D.C.: Government Printing Office, 1889) Series I, 17: 482. James Alex Baggett, ed. *Memories of Madison County* (Jackson, TN: Union University, 1993): 5.
[23] O.R. I, 17: 482-485.

cavalry four miles north of town as he tried to make his way out of West Tennessee. On the 31st, the detachment marched twelve miles north of Lexington to Parker's Crossroads, where it "arrived...just in time to find Forest [*sic*] whiped [*sic*] and retreating." The detachment was ordered to Lexington and then to Jackson, arriving on January 3, 1863.[24] Hurst's second-in-command, Lieutenant Colonel William K.M. Breckenridge, was ordered to prevent Forrest from crossing the Tennessee River at Clifton and escaping back into Middle Tennessee. They skirmished with the advance guard of his cavalry under Colonel George G. Dibrell, but they found themselves almost surrounded and were forced to withdraw. It would not be the last time that the cavalries of Hurst and Forrest would meet during the war.[25]

[24] 6th Tennessee Cavalry Field and Staff Muster Roll, November-December 1862.
[25] Jerry O'Neil Potter, "The First West Tennessee Raid of General Nathan Bedford Forrest." *WTHSP* 28 (1974): 73. Blankenship, *Hurst* 78-79.

Guerrillas In Their Midst

March – May 1863

U NIONISTS WHO HAD SUFFERED at the hands of their Confederate neighbors welcomed the Federal occupation of West Tennessee. Troops concentrated at strategic points along the four railroads that stretched through the region to protect the supply lines vital to the continued invasion of the Confederacy. They also gave protection to the Unionists within their garrisons and enabled them to reorganize and strengthen their numbers without fear of Confederate soldiers or lawless guerrillas.[1]

But deliverance came at a price. The armies that they hoped would bring salvation also brought foraging soldiers who saw little difference between homes and farms owned by Confederates and those of Unionists. Each was plundered of food, horses, mules, livestock, and other necessities in the name of war. Civilians often resorted to hiding them from both armies to ensure their own survival.[2]

The absence of civil authority and the presence of occupation forces gave rise to guerrilla warfare in the region. Guerrillas (or independent partisan rangers) were made up of former soldiers, deserters, and civilians who roamed the countryside exacting their own brand of vigilante justice. Some acted as home guards for their neighborhoods or conscripted able-bodied men for the Confederacy; others engaged in hit-and-run operations to

---

[1] Frisby, "'Homemade Yankees'": 120.
[2] Ibid: 106, 109.

disrupt communications and the flow of supplies to the Union armies. They ambushed patrols and foraging parties, kidnapped civilians and held them for ransom, cut telegraph lines, burnt bridges, and dismantled railroad tracks. When word of their activities filtered back to the post commanders and cavalry was dispatched to pursue them, the guerrillas quickly scattered down side roads and through the woods to elude capture, preferring ambushes to direct frontal attacks.[3] They even disguised themselves in Federal blue uniforms to deceive guards on picket duty, enabling them to come closer and take a shot at them.[4] For the Confederate army, guerrilla warfare became a tool to thwart the Federal presence in the region when they could not. "That mode of warfare seems to be more effective when our forces are so inferior in number to the enemy," wrote one Confederate general."[5]

Though describing conditions in north Mississippi, Brigadier General Gordon Granger gave an insightful description of the frustrations felt by all Federal units forced to combat the guerrilla menace:

> [T]he enemy…know every cowpath and water-hole, and the country is filled with their friends, from whom they can obtain every kind of information as to our whereabouts, movements, and strength. Further, they travel no more on roads unless it is a short distance in the wrong direction to deceive us; shirk about in the night and lie hidden in the day-time. There is no doubt but what every man in this State who has a gun is a guerrilla, and would shoot any of us down whenever he thought it safe to murder us without risking his own neck.[6]

"I hardly know what course to pursue," lamented Major General Stephen A. Hurlbut about the dilemma. "If I send cavalry, they break up and scatter, and my own cavalry commit depredations in following them. The people of the country themselves are more afraid of the guerrillas than of our troops, and therefore will not report them."[7] Many officers believed they should be

---

[3] Grimsley, Mark. *The Hard Hand of War: Union Military Policy toward Southern Civilians, 1861-1865*. (Cambridge, MA: Cambridge University Press, 1995): 111-112.
[4] O.R. I, 24, part 1: 340-341.
[5] Brig. Gen. J.Z. George to Capt. W.A. Goodman, 26 June 1863. O.R. I, 24, part 2: 506. George wrote: "I most respectfully suggest that if our forces be not increased in this district, that most of those we have be employed as guerrillas as far as practicable." Ibid.
[6] O.R. I, 17, part 1: 40.
[7] O.R. I, 24, part 3: 552.

made "serious examples" to the rest of the rebel populace.[8] On July 3, 1862, Major General Ulysses S. Grant decreed "[p]ersons acting as guerrillas without organization and without uniform to distinguish them from private citizens are not entitled to the treatment of prisoners of war when caught, and will not receive such treatment."[9]

As military commander of Memphis, Major General William Tecumseh Sherman initiated a policy of collective punishment in the summer of 1862 to combat the guerrillas and the civilians who protected them. Rather than exhaust troops and cavalry searching the countryside for the perpetrators, he advocated the arrest or expulsion of prominent secessionist from the locality or burning their homes and property. He concluded that it was the local secessionists who supported the guerrillas and that their support would stop if it were their own lives and property that were threatened with retaliation.[10] In areas that were rampant with guerrilla activity, Sherman vowed to heavily forage upon their homes and farms for food, horses, wagons, and other items useful to the military. "If the people do not want [them]…taken, they must organize and repress all guerrillas or hostile bands in their neighborhood," he reasoned.[11]

Guerrillas also terrorized Unionists, hoping to drive them away from their neighborhoods. Some families were forced to leave their homes and move north to Paducah, Kentucky or across the Ohio River into southern Illinois, Indiana, and Ohio for the duration of the war; others stubbornly refused to leave and endured the threats against their homes, their property, and their lives. Ineffective as they were in the backwoods, the occupational armies were still their only defense. Major General Henry W. Halleck acknowledged that giving up any part of West Tennessee would be "certain death to all Union men in that territory."[12]

In January 1863, Colonel John Kemp Mizner went so far as to declare that for every loyal citizen apprehended by guerrillas in Haywood and Tipton counties, he would do the same to two secessionists from a list of fourteen names in his possession. The same "eye for an eye" principle would be applied in retaliation for property damage against Unionist

---

[8] Ibid. O.R. I, 24, part 3: 111.

[9] O.R. I, 17, part 2: 69.

[10] Noel C. Fisher, "'Prepare Them For My Coming': General William T. Sherman, Total War, and Pacification in West Tennessee." *Tennessee Historical Quarterly* 51.2: 78-83.

[11] O.R. I, 31, part 1: 731. Fisher, "'Prepare Them For My Coming'": 81-82.

[12] O.R. I, 16, part 3: 82.

citizens. Guerrilla leader Colonel Richard V. Richardson countered "this paper bullet fired across the Hatchie River by the brave Colonel Mizner" with the promise that for every Confederate citizen arrested in the same counties, he would shoot "twice the number of Yankee soldiers" and "for each dollar's worth of property taken...I will take or destroy twice the amount from the United States, their soldiers and Union men." Richardson made his own vow that "for every house burned by the U.S. soldiers I will shoot five U.S. soldiers on duty or taken in battle."[13] Three months later, Major General Hurlbut ordered that Richardson and his gang "must be exterminated, and the sooner the better."[14]

Unlike their Northern comrades whose families were safely away from the fighting, the soldiers of the 6th Tennessee feared for their loved ones at home. Throughout the war, Hurst pressed his superiors to station the regiment closer to them, many living in the counties along the Tennessee River, and allow his men "some chance to provide for their families."[15] But guerrillas were not their only threat. Hurst's home had been "once Robed [sic] by the Rebels and three times by the d—d Ill[inois] troops who have more sympathy for a Rebel than they have for a loyal man in Tennessee."[16]

William C. Hughes acted as a recruiter and informant for the regiment and his intelligence often helped Colonel Hurst determined the movements of his command. His activities and his Unionist sentiments made Hughes fear returning to his home in Hardin County. On October 3, 1863, a group of guerrillas went there determined to kill either Hughes or his wife Winnie; because he was not there, she was shot and killed. His daughter almost died after one of them hit her on the head with his gun as she bent down to help her mother. With his farm stripped of its crops and livestock and his wife dead, Hughes decided to move his children north to southern Illinois for the remainder of the war.[17]

One notable guerrilla leader who operated in West Tennessee and North Mississippi during this period was Solomon G. Street.[18] Officially, Street was

---

13 O.R. II, 5: 821.

14 O.R. I, 24, part 3: 111.

15 Hurst to Andrew Johnson, 11 March 1863. RLB.

16 Hurst to Maj. W.H. Morgan, 15 September 1864. Hurst Military Records.

17 William C. Hughes SCC No. 17798.

18 Solomon G. Street (1832-1864) was born in Hardeman County, Tennessee. The 1860 Census for Tippah County, Mississippi showed he was a 29-year-old tanner with a wife and two young children. Tommy Lockhart, Bill Gurney, and W. Fred Cox. "1860 Census of Tippah County, Mississippi." July

captain of Company A in the Second Mississippi Cavalry, a home guard unit for the state of Mississippi but not part of the Confederate army; Union authorities came to know him as Sol Street "of guerrilla notoriety."[19] In August 1862, Street returned to his home in Tippah County, Mississippi after serving a year in the Army of Northern Virginia and organized his own irregular command of former Confederate soldiers and civilians. He also utilized Captain W.H. Wilson's Company D and other north Mississippi home guard units on his raids.[20]

As early as December 1862, Street and his command were among the various guerrilla factions that harassed Union forces in the region. Brigadier General Mason Brayman loathed them as a pestilence that "infest the neighborhood" around his post, "carrying away citizens, stealing horses, and subsisting by plunder." He was confident they could be eliminated if he had "a small efficient cavalry" to "drive them from their haunts" along the bends of the Hatchie River in the vicinity of Somerville. But he had none, he conceded; all he could do was guard the immediate vicinity and provide escorts for the foraging parties that went into the countryside.[21]

While Major Daniel M. Emerson and a squad of the 1st West Tennessee Cavalry were on an expedition to find the guerrillas, a group of fifteen under Street found them south of Bolivar on January 25, 1863. The guerrillas—partially dressed in Federal blue uniforms—fired upon their rear and captured one private who fell from his horse. Emerson wheeled his men around to confront them but after a two-mile chase on horseback, Street's men dispersed into the dense woods and eluded capture. Unbeknownst to Emerson, the guerrillas camped not far away from his command that night but did not attack. Still, the expedition was not a complete loss: it apprehended two Confederate officers of the 22nd Tennessee Infantry on a recruitment trip to Shelby County and two privates who were home on furlough.[22]

12, 2007. <www.rootsweb.com/~mstippah/1860-s.html> He was shot and killed by a 16-year-old Confederate soldier named Robert Galloway. The motive was Street had robbed his father or burned his cotton to keep it out of Union hands. Andrew Brown, "Sol Street, Confederate Partisan Leader." <www.rootsweb.com/~mscivilw/solstreet.htm>

[19] Brown, "Street": n.p. O.R. I, 24 (part 1): 334.

[20] Brown, "Street."

[21] O.R. I, 17, part 1: 482, 485.

[22] O.R. I, 24, part 1: 331-332.

In February, Street drew the ire of Colonel Hurst and the 1st West Tennessee after eight members of the regiment were killed on picket duty over a period of time. When Hurst took a small squad from the garrison one night to hunt for him, the attack stopped; once he returned to the post at midnight, the shooting resumed. The next morning, Hurst and a larger detachment of 100 soldiers pursued them and eventually caught up with them outside Saulsbury, Tennessee. There was a skirmish and eight guerrillas were captured along with several carbines and horses. During the fight, the bullet from a guerrilla's gun actually lodged inside the muzzle of Hurst's revolver; "one half variation would have blown his brains out," recalled his quartermaster, William J. Smith.[23]

A governmental payroll aboard a poorly guarded train presented Sol Street with the opportunity for his most daring foray. He learned that a train from Bolivar would bring payments to laborers working on the Mississippi Central Railroad at Grand Junction. He collaborated with Captain W.H. Wilson to disable the track three and a half miles north of Grand Junction and capture the valuable cargo. On the morning of March 21, eighty guerrillas waited in the woods along both sides of the track at a sharp curve where they had removed one of the rails. But a construction train preceded the payroll train and derailed when it reached the curve, knocking its engine, tender, and five cars off the tracks. Believing it to be the payroll train, the guerrillas sprang from the woods and captured the engineer and passengers, including sixteen African-Americans. But the real object of their sabotage realized what was happening and the engineer stopped his train and threw the locomotive into reverse. Amid a hail of bullets that pelted its iron shell, the payroll train steamed back up the track to safety. Street and his men were left with thirty-two prisoners but no Federal currency for their efforts.[24]

The 1st West Tennessee Cavalry was ordered from Bolivar to find Street's command, which Brigadier General Brayman believed had traveled northwest of the railroad toward Somerville. Colonel Hurst searched along the railroad south to Middleburg and west toward Whiteville but could not track them down.[25] The Sixth Illinois Cavalry was dispatched from La Grange to Saulsbury for the same purpose. Having learned that Street's

---

[23] Memphis *Bulletin*, March 4, 1863. Frisby, "'Homemade Yankees'": 171.

[24] O.R. I, 24, part 1: 470-471. Brown, "Street."

[25] O.R. I, 24, part 1: 471.

command had split into three groups with several hours' head start, they abandoned the pursuit.[26]

According to one account, Hurst and a detachment of the 1st West Tennessee ventured further south than their commanding officer knew. On the morning of March 22, they rode into Ripley, Mississippi about forty miles south of Grand Junction where they seized horses and confiscated bales of cotton from local residents. They also captured four men, one of whom was a private in the 7th Mississippi Cavalry.[27] Colonel John H. Miller, a Presbyterian minister who was organizing cavalry regiments in Tippah County, was apprehended and murdered two miles south of Ripley by two soldiers of the 1st West Tennessee. They took from him various personal effects, about fifty or sixty dollars—even his false teeth and the sermon he intended to preach that Sabbath day—and left his body in the road. The soldiers claimed he resisted arrest but one witness refuted it and said he had surrendered.[28]

The regiment left Ripley and made their way back across the state line toward the Union post at Pocahontas, Tennessee. By this time, Sol Street and his command were back in north Mississippi and hoped to reclaim some of the horses and cotton Hurst had taken. On March 24, the guerrillas rushed ahead of them off the main road through the bottoms of Muddy Creek and a mile south of Jonesborough, Mississippi, where one detachment of Street's men captured eight soldiers in the 1st West Tennessee's rear guard. Street and the rest of his command galloped across the state line and positioned themselves a mile and a half south of Pocahontas and ahead of the 1st West Tennessee. The guerrillas charged but soon found themselves outnumbered and their gunpowder wet from trudging through the creek bottoms.[29] Hurst believed it was he who was outnumbered and rushed a plea for reinforcements over the telegraph wire to Brigadier General Brayman at Bolivar, overestimating the enemy's strength at 400.[30] Street

26 Ibid: 471-472.
27 Judge Orlando Davis Diary, March 22, 1863 entry. <www.rootsweb.com/%7emscivilw/davis.htm> Richmond (VA) Daily Dispatch, May 2, 1863. Brown, "Street." The men who were arrested were D. W. Rogers, Bob Smith, Charles McCarley, and a man named Dickson. Only McCarley could be confirmed as a Confederate soldier. Civil War Soldiers and Sailors System.
28 Richmond (VA) Daily Dispatch, May 2, 1863. Orlando Davis accused a Lieutenant Mooney and an unknown member of the 1st West Tennessee Cavalry for the murder. Only one Mooney served in the regiment and that was Private John Mooney of Company C. Davis diary.
29 Brown, "Street."
30 O.R. I, 24, part 3: 137.

soon withdrew back into Mississippi but left behind twenty-eight of his men who were sent as prisoners to the Union posts at Bethel Station and Bolivar. Hurst erroneously reported that Street himself had been "desperately wounded." The 1st West Tennessee suffered only one loss in the engagement.[31]

A few weeks later, one hundred and seventy-five soldiers and eleven officers from the regiment, including Colonel Hurst, joined an expedition with the 18th Illinois Mounted Infantry under the command of Colonel Michael Kelly Lawler. The sixteen-day campaign along the Hatchie River in April resulted in the capture of forty-three guerrillas, including four officers, two surgeons, and twenty-eight men belonging to Colonel Richard V. Richardson's command, along with 110 horses and mules.[32] They were told by Unionists in Tipton and Haywood counties that Richardson had robbed civilians there and in other southwest Tennessee counties and had fled across the Mississippi River with his loot. Having learned that some men under Richardson's command were upset with their leader's thievery, Lawler offered them amnesty if they surrendered their arms, swore an oath of allegiance to the United States, and returned peacefully to their homes. Otherwise they would be held "responsible for any act or deeds perpetrated by such bands."[33]

Among the prisoners captured during the expedition was Lieutenant Colonel James U. Green of Richardson's 12th Tennessee (C.S.) Cavalry. He related his encounter with Colonel Hurst and the 1st West Tennessee Cavalry after the war:

> I mentioned [to Hurst] that my canteen contained some whisky, and he ordered it returned to me; but the whisky was gone. He cussed his men [as] "a set of thieves." Then he ordered his own canteen, and we drank— he, to the Stars and Stripes, and I, to the "Stars and Bars." We took supper together, and he and I were bedfellows for the night, lying in the bed in which I hid my pistol just before surrendering.[34]

Green also recalled a fellow prisoner, a civilian named Jamison, who Hurst scrutinized "for being a Rebel and not in the army." The defiant old

---

[31] O.R. I, 24, part 3: 147.

[32] O.R. I, 24, part 1: 498.

[33] Ibid: 499.

[34] "Prison Life and Escape of Col. Green." *Confederate Veteran* 7.1 (January 1899): 57

man angrily replied, "Turn me loose, Col. Hurst, and if I don't get a gun and shoot you the next time you come through Tipton, you may carry me to prison and keep me there until I rot." He set Jamison free, perhaps amused by such a bold threat from an old man.[35]

On the journey back to Bolivar, Hurst allowed Green to ride his horse, as the one Green had was "a shabby steed." The kind treatment ended, however, once the expedition reached the Union post. Major William J. Smith of the 1st West Tennessee "robbed us of our overcoats and blankets," Green remembered, and "shut [us] up in a brick storeroom for the night."[36]

Hurst found himself in enemy hands when two members of Colonel Richard V. Richardson's group captured him four miles southwest of Somerville, Tennessee on July 25. While on scout with a squad of the 1st West Tennessee, he stopped for a moment to talk with a widow named Lewis and her daughter at their front gate as he waited for some of his men to rejoin him. Two Confederate soldiers named Hugh Nelson and C.A.S. Shaw, returning home to Somerville for fresh horses and clothing, came upon Hurst on the road. They approached him from behind with guns drawn as Mrs. Lewis asked, "Col[onel] ain't you afraid the Rebels will catch you[?]"[37] No sooner had he replied that he wasn't when the two soldiers took his pistols from his saddle holsters and led him away on horseback toward their encampment.[38] Hurst knew his men would try and find him and he rode slowly between his captors to give them more time to catch up. When they objected to his pace, he told them they could shoot him if they did not like it.[39]

Meanwhile Captain Harry Hodges of Company B and a group of eight soldiers from the regiment had pursued them for seven miles. When they were found, Lieutenant Risden D. Deford and an African-American servant belonging to Captain Robert M. Thompson of Company A ran ahead and

---

[35] Ibid.

[36] Ibid.

[37] Christopher W. Robertson Civil War Questionnaire at TSLA. Christopher W. Robertson to John Trotwood Moore, May 15, 1922

[38] In his communication to Brig. Gen. Grenville M. Dodger on July 28, 1863, Col. John K. Mizner claimed his capture "resulted from his mistaking two of the enemy for his own men while detached from the main column." O.R. I, 24, part 3: 559.

[39] Memphis *Bulletin*, August 5, 1863. Robertson to Moore, May 15, 1922. Ibid.

began firing at them.[40] In the confusion, Hurst "drew rein and turned his quick grey mare" into the woods as one of his captors shot at him with one of his own pistols.[41] Hodges gave Hurst a revolver and the 1st West Tennessee chased the Confederate soldiers to within a few hundred feet of Richardson's encampment. Outnumbered, Hurst and his men turned back a short distance to the top of a hill where they were joined by the rest of the squad. They "cheered lustily, making so much noise that the Rebels thought the whole regiment was coming to avenge their Colonel's wrongs." Richardson's command was tempted but grudgingly decided to give up their trophy without a fight.[42]

The Memphis *Bulletin* initially reported that Hurst had been killed. "[H]is cowardly captors, seeing that they could not escape with him, shot eleven balls into his body, which they left for a corpse," it claimed.[43] A correction was published the next day when it was learned that Colonel Hurst had instead escaped from "the notorious horse-thief Richardson." He "is yet in the land of the living," opined the *Bulletin*, "and will yet make the prowling bands of rebel bushwhackers who have been annoying the citizens, feel his prowess."[44] His superior officer and chief of cavalry Colonel John K. Mizner hoped Hurst had learned not to leave the protection of his cavalry again. "I think his experience will be an advantage to him," he wrote.[45]

Mrs. Lewis and her neighbors paid a heavy price for the incident. Committing Major General Sherman's policy of collective punishment to practice, the 1st West Tennessee returned to the area, foraged on their farms, and burned their homes to the ground. One elderly woman was physically removed from her home and placed in a corncrib as they set her residence ablaze. When Mrs. Lewis' 16-year-old son returned home to find its charred remains, he vowed, "I'll be d—d if this hasn't made me a Soldier," and enlisted in the Confederate army.[46]

By September 1863, the guerrilla bands of Solomon G. Street and Richard V. Richardson had been legitimized and brought into the Confederate army under Brigadier General Stephen D. Lee. Street was captured along

[40] Memphis *Bulletin*, August 5, 1863.
[41] Robertson CWQ.
[42] Memphis *Bulletin*, August 5, 1863.
[43] Memphis *Bulletin*, July 30, 1863.
[44] Memphis *Bulletin*, July 31, 1863
[45] O.R. I, 24, part 3: 559.
[46] Ibid.

with fifty-five of his men during a conscription campaign through West Tennessee and western Kentucky on November 20.[47] Like his nemesis Colonel Hurst, he managed to escape and rejoin his command. His battalion was incorporated into the 15th Tennessee (C.S.) Cavalry on January 25, 1864 and became part of Nathan Bedford Forrest's Cavalry Department with Street attaining the rank of major.[48] But his thievery as a guerrilla eventually caught up with him. He was later shot and killed by a 16-year-old Confederate recruit named Robert Galloway to avenge his father who had been robbed and murdered by Street.[49]

---

[47] O.R. I, 31, part 3: 570.

[48] Brown, "Street." Henry, *First with the Most*: 214.

[49] John Milton Hubbard, *Notes of a Private* (Memphis, TN: E.H. Clarke & Brother, 1909): 88-89. Brown, "Street."

SUCH WHOLESALE AND WANTON DESTRUCTION

APRIL – JULY 1863

D ESPITE SEVEN MONTHS OF MILITARY SERVICE, the government that the 1st West Tennessee Cavalry fought to defend had still not officially recognized its contributions. The War Department had not paid its soldiers and provided them with no firearms and only 100 "worn out" saddles. Its soldiers drilled, scouted, and picketed with their own personal weapons and horses in the face of "jeers and jibes at the folly of working for nothing" by their Northern counterparts and "often suffered for comforts, and luxuries, enjoyed by others" in the army.[1]

Colonel Hurst continued to seek help from Military Governor Andrew Johnson but like his men, he too had become frustrated with the lack of support and appreciation. He requested 250 guns but had been told he first needed a complete regiment. Yet he could not recruit additional men because he had been stationed "in the midst of Rebeldom" at Bolivar, Tennessee. Knowing their families were suffering back home only made their circumstances worse. "What must I do If I have no Regiment and I [am] not entitled to Recruit where I think proper[?]" he asked Johnson. "I want orders and instructions from you[.] My men feel that they have been badly treated[.] No pay and but little thanks[.]"[2]

---

[1] Hurst to Johnson, 11 March 1863. RLB. Memphis *Bulletin*, 31 July 31 1863.
[2] Hurst to Johnson, 11 March 1863. RLB.

Two companies were added to the 1st West Tennessee and mustered into service on March 7, 1863. Company G elected William Chandler, related by marriage to Colonel Hurst, as its first captain and Captain Joseph G. Berry became the leader of Company H. Both were organized with volunteers largely from Decatur, Hardin, Perry, and Wayne counties.[3]

During an expedition to Purdy, Tennessee on April 16, 1863, Hurst learned that two horses belonging to him ("the only pair of horses in town," claimed one resident) had been stolen. In his mind, it was sufficient reason to burn the homes of local Confederate sympathizers.[4] He ordered them to remove their furniture and belongings before he set their homes on fire. The McNairy County Courthouse was spared and the son of the county court clerk recalled that Hurst refused to let his men confiscate the record books.[5] Upon returning home from out of state, William S. Wisdom, one of its wealthiest citizens, found "the town was afire & not a citizen could say a word lest the bayonet would be his portion." His brick home was also in line for the torch. But Wisdom's wife interceded with Hurst's wife, who in turn convinced her husband to spare it. Residents not as fortunate as the Wisdoms were left homeless and forced to seek shelter in local churches and at Purdy College.[6]

At one point during the war, two regiments of Nathan Bedford Forrest's cavalry rode through Purdy and found "blackened walls, lone chimneys, and charred remains of buildings." Forrest feared that his soldiers who lived in the area might seek vengeance by burning Hurst's home. He placed a guard to protect it, much to the appreciation of Melocky Hurst.[7]

Colonel E.W. Rice, post commander at Bethel Station, learned what Hurst had done but did not "know by what authority" he did it.[8] Rice informed Major General Richard Oglesby, who in turn ordered Brigadier General Nathan Kimball to "ascertain by what authority Col. Hurst is on this expedition and why he is thus destroying property. If [it is] upon

---

3 TITCW 1:333

4 Emma Inman Williams, ed. "Hettie Wisdom Tapp's Memoirs." *WTHSP* 36 (1982): 123. Tapp claimed the horses were stolen by two Union soldiers who deserted from their unit. Ibid.

5 Jeff Walker, "Early History of McNairy County." *McNairy County Independent*, November 23, 1923.

6 Williams, "Memoirs": 123. "William S. Wisdom." *McNairy County Independent*, 11 January 1924. Another resident, Dr. Daniel Barry, was also fortunate to have his home spared. Barry, "A Long Time Ago." *McNairy County Independent*, 18 January 1924.

7 "Gen. Forrest Among Civilians." *Confederate Veteran* 3.4 (April 1895): 106.

8 Col. E.W. Rice to Maj. Gen. Richard Oglesby, 16 April 1863. Hurst Military Records.

authority from Genl Brayman you will order his return to Bolivar, and require an explanation of his conduct."[9]

When Hurst returned to Bolivar on April 19, he brought with him an order for his arrest issued by Ogelsby and Brayman complied. Brayman also learned that Hurst had encouraged his men to desert. He was forced to send search parties to find those who had left the post after nightfall. Brayman blamed their conduct on the War Department for not paying them. "Unless this reg[imen]t can be mustered and paid [and] recognized as Soldiers," he wrote Kimball, "I think their continuance in their present relation to the Service, [would be] injurious to all concerned."[10] It was not until July 23 that the men of the 1st West Tennessee Cavalry finally received their first payments.[11]

A daring and successful expedition for the regiment took place on the evening of May 12. A detachment of fifty-five soldiers under Lieutenant Colonel William K.M. Breckenridge disembarked from a gunboat on the east bank of the Tennessee River and, according to the official report, "dashed across country to Linden [and] surprised [a] rebel force, more than twice its number." Thirty-seven Rebels were captured, among them a lieutenant colonel and ten conscripted soldiers, as well as fifty horses and two wagons. They also set fire to the Perry County Courthouse, which was being used as an armory for Confederate munitions and supplies. The group suffered no losses and the prisoners were transported to Cairo, Illinois.[12]

On the morning of July 12, 1863, Colonel Hurst and 200 soldiers of the 1st West Tennessee Cavalry marched with the 3rd Michigan Cavalry and 2nd Iowa Cavalry on an expedition to Jackson, Tennessee. Led by Colonel Edward Hatch[13], commander of the Second Cavalry Brigade, they left

9 Ibid.
10 Mason Brayman to E.C. Mason, April 20, 1863 in Hurst Military Records.
11 Memphis *Bulletin*, July 31, 1863.
12 O.R. I, 23, part 1: 331.
13 Edward Hatch (1832-1889) was commissioned as a captain in the 2nd Iowa Cavalry on August 12, 1861. He was promoted to colonel ten months later. He participated in Benjamin H. Grierson's raid from LaGrange, Tennessee through Mississippi to Baton Rogue, Louisiana and upon that officer's recommendation, he was promoted to brigadier general. During a raid in Oxford, Mississippi, former

Bolivar and camped fourteen miles away on the Denmark Road. The next morning, they were met by the 9th Illinois Infantry and continued toward Jackson. Hatch instructed Hurst to take his force along the Woodville Road, the only route that still had bridges across the Forked Deer River. The rest of the expedition marched into town on the Brownsville Road.[14]

The expedition engaged Confederate forces under Colonels Jesse A. Forrest, N.N. Cox and John F. Newsom in and around Jackson the entire day. The Rebels were forced to withdraw as night approached but the Federals were unable to pursue due to foggy conditions. The next day, Hatch learned that the Confederates had retreated toward the Tennessee River and he sent units to pursue them, with Hurst and his command marching north toward Lexington.[15]

Eight miles from Jackson on the morning of the 14th, the 1st West Tennessee encountered the rebel cavalry they were sent to pursue. The enemy "fled before us in great hast[e]," reported Hurst, "destroying all the bridges they crossed." The unit captured twenty prisoners, eight of whom they paroled but they returned with only seven. Five escaped, he explained, due to his "rear guard being worn out with fatigue from hard marching and crossing streams by fording Swimming &c." The Rebels were "in a badly torn up and demoralized condition and would have been easily Cap-tured...[as] they were out of ammunition and low Spirited."[16]

During and after the fighting stragglers from the Union expedition broke into local homes and businesses, robbing and burning them. In his report, Colonel Hatch confessed that soldiers under his command discovered "thirty barrels of whiskey" that they confiscated and consumed, giving him "as much trouble [trying to] save the town from fire during the fight as it did to whip the enemy...The stores, I regret to say, were plundered by negroes and stragglers during the fight."[17] Resident Robert H. Cartmell recorded in his diary that stores "were broken open and such destruction I

Secretary of the Interior Jacob Thompson blamed him for the plundering of his home and belongings there. Warner, *Generals in Blue*. 215-216.

[14] WOTR 1, 24, part 2: 674-676.

[15] O.R. I, 24, part 2: 673-675.

[16] O.R. I, 24, part 2: 682.

[17] O.R. I, 24, part 2: 675.

never saw…'Twas sickening to look at such wholesale and wanton destruction."[18]

One store in particular, a millinery shop owned by Mrs. A.A. Newman, a British citizen, was especially vandalized. She complained to the Union authorities at Memphis that soldiers of the 1st West Tennessee Cavalry broke into her business, stole her merchandise, and even took her bonnets to decorate the heads of their horses. An investigation was conducted in the fall of 1863 and Colonel Hurst and officers of the regiment gave their accounts of the events that day. Lieutenant Colonel Breckenridge gave his report on September 28:

> Our regiment was in the rear, and, after crossing the [Forked Deer] river, I was ordered to take charge of all the wagons and led horses, as the men were mostly dismounted, and as the command advanced I moved the lead horses until I arrived at the edge of town. I there received an order from an orderly to take charge of the prisoners and picket the town. I then rode up to the court-house, where the prisoners were, and while there a citizen came to me and reported that citizens were carrying out whiskey by the bucket-full and giving it to the men, and I rode over to where they were and had the whiskey all spilled that I could find. I then went to where my reserve was, and sent Lieutenant [Samuel] Lewis with 10 men to destroy all the liquor they could find. In a short time he came to me and said that the men were breaking into the houses, and I ordered him to go and stop them, and to arrest every man he found in a house. He then went off, and in a short time returned and told me of Mrs. A.A. Newman's millinery shop or store, and I ordered him to put a guard over the house…after dark, I and another officer of the command…heard a noise at a door and scouted to see about it, and on the way I found about 30 men, I suppose, in and in front of a store. He said they belonged to his regiment, and I ordered them out…in a few minutes [I] returned; they were trying to get in again. I sent the officer to send them off, and I spent most of my time that night in running from place to place trying to keep

---

[18] Emma Inman Williams, *Historic Madison: The Story of Jackson and Madison County, Tennessee, from the Prehistoric Moundbuilders to 1917* (Jackson, TN: Madison County Historical Society, 1946): 178.

everything quiet and seeing the wounded. And in the morning, when Colonel Hatch returned to town, the men broke open houses and took all they wanted, and took buggies and wagons and loaded them with goods and boats, &c. I stood in the court-house yard and saw a portion of his command pass, and nearly every man had something that had been taken out of the place.[19]

Lieutenant Samuel Lewis' report, dated October 4, recalled that while "searching for whiskey [to destroy], I went into one millinery store belonging to a widow lady, and found her very much excited about the soldiers carrying out her goods. She demanded of me a guard. I went to [Lieutenant] Colonel Breckenridge and related her circumstances to him, and he told me to give her a guard." After talking with Colonel Hurst about the looting, he remembered: "I saw Colonel Hatch's men, of the 3rd Michigan, or the 2nd Iowa Cavalry, breaking open store-house doors and carrying out goods of almost every description."[20]

Hurst's report, also dated October 4, elaborated:

I was ordered to report to Col[onel] Hatch in Town. When I reached the [court] square I saw the fire near Mrs. Newman's shop. I asked Col[onel] Breckenridge what the fire meant. He said Hatches [sic] men were burning up clothing. I abused such Conduct [and] some one who I believe was (a) Lieut[enant] in the 2nd Iowa said yes it was wrong but the boys said it was nearly all secesh Clothing [sic]. I ordered my men to remain on their horses and let the Town alone which they did as far as I saw.[21]

Hurst blamed members of the 3rd Michigan Cavalry "and perhaps some of the 2nd Iowa" for ransacking the town. They "broke every door shutter in sight," he wrote, with "their officers making Sport by saying them Damed [sic] Horses would kick the town to pieces if [they] were not moved." Calling Colonel Hatch's attention to the fires being started, he claimed the Union officer "spoke of it in Indifference." Hurst added: "The citizens said to me that my men had acted the Gentlemen with them, but Col[onel] Hatch let his men do too bad."[22]

---

[19] O.R. I, 24, part 2: 679.

[20] O.R. I, 24, part 2: 679-680.

[21] O.R. I, 24, part 2: 682.

[22] O.R. I, 24, part 2: 679-680. Hurst to Edward Hatch, October 4, 1863. Regimental Letter Book.

But Hurst was hardly a gentleman. While at a local hospital, he allegedly cursed a young woman who said something he didn't like. "[H]e became furious," wrote Robert H. Cartmell, and "called the lady a d—d slut and told her if she did not get out, he would kick her out…I heard those present repeat his language and worse than I have written. This is truly a war upon private citizens and private property."[23]

Despite the regiment's version of the events at Jackson, the verdict of the military authorities blamed the vandalism of the millinery store solely upon the 1st West Tennessee Cavalry. Mrs. Newman was awarded $5,139.25 in damages, which was deducted from the regiment's payroll.[24] Hurst would not forget what he felt was an injustice against himself and his command. The residents of Jackson had not seen the last of him or his regiment.

A few days later, members of the 1st West Tennessee skirmished with a squad of four soldiers from Colonel Andrew N. Wilson's Tennessee Cavalry regiment led by Captain John Ambrose "Dock" Wharton[25] near Purdy. Colonel Hurst believed them to be guerrillas rather than Confederate soldiers. During the fight, Wharton was wounded and his men were captured. He was taken to Hurst, who claimed the Confederate captain "had been seeking his life" and Hurst decided to take Wharton's life instead. Wharton vowed that "if you kill me 10 of your men will go up for me," implying they would be hanged for his death. He and his men were shot and killed and their bodies left on the road leading from Purdy to Pocahontas.[26] One of them, a twenty-four-year-old from Alabama named Thomas W.S. Morgan, was left to die. The Locke family that lived nearby heard his cries

---

[23] Williams, *Historic Madison*: 72.

[24] Blankenship, *Hurst*: 79-80.

[25] John Ambrose Wharton (circa 1836-1863) was one of five brothers who fought for the Confederacy. He initially served in Company F of the 13th Tennessee Infantry and was severely wounded at Shiloh. Later he was made a captain in Wilson's Tennessee Cavalry. Wharton family history courtesy of Lane Wharton. Dew M. Wisdom to Col. Philip D. Roddey, 23 July 1863. NARA M474, RG 109, Reel 88, Frames 167-169 (National Archives). "Wilson's Tennessee Cavalry Regiment." TNGenWeb Tennesseans in the Civil War Project. <www.tngenweb.com/civil war/csacav/csawilson.html>

[26] Wisdom to Roddey, 23 July 1863. The four men with Wharton were George Brown, Hugh Hollis, Thomas W.S. Morgan, and Thomas Starks. Ibid. Wharton and his men are blamed for the murder of Fielding Hurst's nephew, William Hurst, in Blankenship, "Fielding Hurst": 83. This is not the case; refer to footnote 20 on page 67 for a further explanation.

and nursed him as best they could, but they feared that taking him into their home would anger Hurst and his men. There he died and was buried.[27]

Lieutenant Colonel Dew M. Wisdom of Wilson's command, the son of a wealthy McNairy County family, learned of the executions and reported them to Colonel Philip D. Roddey. "Can not [Wharton's] words be verified, and 10 men be slain for him[?] Is it not a case for retaliation[?]" pleaded Wisdom.[28] Roddey forwarded the letter to Confederate Secretary of War James A. Seddon, who in turn sent it to Jefferson Davis. The Confederate president authorized General Braxton Bragg, commander of the Army of Tennessee, to investigate the matter. If proved to be true, he ordered Bragg to "adopt such retaliatory measures" as required "without awaiting specific instructions."[29]

According to legend, for each mile passed on the road, a prisoner was executed and his body buried alongside the road as a mile marker.[30] A more gruesome version claimed they were decapitated and their heads placed on top of the actual mile markers.[31] Wisdom's letter is the sole extant source for information on the Wharton incident and does not mention such a pattern of executions or barbaric displays.

Despite Fielding Hurst's cruel reputation, there were also stories of his kindness toward prisoners such as the one related by Lieutenant Colonel James U. Green. Another involved Major Nathaniel F. Cheairs, a member of Nathan Bedford Forrest's Commissary Department. He had been ordered to secure cattle for the Confederate army in West Tennessee by

[27] *Reflections*: 221-222. The land was owned by Daniel Locke and had been farmed by his son Robert H. Locke until his enlistment in Company A of the 6th Tennessee Cavalry. Ibid: 221. The tombstone, located in the Byrdall community of McNairy County, reads: "Thomas W.S./son of J.R. and L. Morgan/was/murdered/1863/Aged About/24 Years." Ibid.

[28] Wisdom to Roddey, 23 July 1863.

[29] O.R. II, 6: 202-203. Lynda Lasswell Crist, ed. *The Papers of Jefferson Davis*. Vol. 9. (Baton Rogue: Louisiana State University Press, 1997): 335.

[30] Williams, *Historic Madison*: 178. Blankenship, "Hurst" *WTHP* 34 (Oct. 1980): 83. Miss Williams was the first historian to suggest that Hurst "killed one every mile and buried them as mile posts." Her conclusion was based on her citation of Confederate Secretary of War James A. Seddon's letter to Gen. Braxton Bragg on 14 August 1863 (O.R. II, 6:202-203). But the letter states only that Wharton and his men were murdered "on the road from Purdy to Pocahontas" It does not mention their bodies being intentionally buried as mile posts.

[31] W. Clay Cook, "Hurst!" <www.hurstnation.com> Cook does not cite the source of this version.

General Joseph E. Johnston. His first attempt failed, he explained to Johnston, because "Colonel Fielding Hurst is in there with a regiment of thieves and highway robbers" who committed "all sorts of devilment. There is no chance of getting supplies of any kind." Still, he was ordered to return and was captured with two companions by members of Company K of the 6th Tennessee Cavalry six miles outside Brownsville.[32]

The prisoners were brought before an impromptu drumhead court-martial presided over by Fielding Hurst. They were charged with spying and bushwhacking activities, found guilty, and sentenced to be executed the following morning. On his way to his quarters, Cheairs talked with Captain Albert Cook of Company K and realized that he knew Cook's uncle who was the town marshal in Columbia, Tennessee. Both men also belonged to fraternal Masonic societies, as did Hurst. Cook sympathized with Cheairs' plight and offered him advice about his commanding officer. Hurst had "a heart as tender as a woman…if you approach him right," he said. "If you don't, he is the damnest, meanest man that God ever made."[33]

Cheairs secured an audience with Hurst later that evening. "We found Col. Hurst and his Major playing cards with two women they were dragging over the country in carriages they had taken from Southern sympathizers," he recalled. "Are you the man that wants to see me?" asked Hurst. Cheairs said that he was. After asking the major to escort the ladies upstairs, Hurst inquired what Cheairs wanted from him. The prisoner said they had met before the war at the Masonic Grand Lodge in Nashville and mentioned a "gross masonic offense" committed by a member of Hurst's home lodge. Hurst was convinced of his truthfulness and waived the death sentence, but he would not do so for his non-Masonic companions. Cheairs declined his pardon without them, an act that stirred Hurst who "with tears trickling down his face" revoked their death sentences as well.[34]

---

[32] Nathaniel Cheairs, "Personal Experiences in the Civil War." Civil War Collection, Account No. 1252, Box 1, Folder 5 at TSLA.

[33] Ibid.

[34] Ibid.

By order of the War Department, Companies A, B, C, D and E of Lieutenant Colonel Isaac R. Hawkins' 1st West Tennessee Infantry were taken from his command and added to the 1st West Tennessee Cavalry. This consolidation increased its size to eleven companies. The order was issued on May 14 but it was not until July 1 that they were officially mustered into the regiment by a Lieutenant Hoffman at LaGrange, Tennessee. They were designated as Companies I, K, L, and M.[35]

Company I was originally organized at Dresden, Tennessee in June 1862 with Orlando H. Shearer as captain; Company K at Dresden in July 1862, Thomas H. Boswell captain; Company L at Dresden in July 1862, John H. Edwards captain; and Company M at North Gibson, Tennessee (now Skullbone) in August 1862, William Carroll Holt captain. The new units consisted of men from Gibson and Weakley counties. Their addition to the regiment entitled it to another major and Hurst nominated Captain Boswell of Company K. Albert Cook replaced him as captain.[36]

The 1st West Tennessee was also given a new designation. With confusion arising from too many "1st Tennessee" regiments operating in the state (it being one of six such commands), the state adjutant general renumbered them. In June 1863 the 1st West Tennessee Cavalry became known as the 6th Tennessee Cavalry.[37]

---

[35] Fielding Hurst to Andrew Johnson, 31 July 1863. RLB.

[36] Hurst to Johnson, 20 August 1863. RLB. TICW: 333-334.

[37] Current, *Lincoln's Loyalists*: 59. "What Tennessee Loyalists Have Done." Memphis *Bulletin*, 5 August 1863: 1.

A FIELD OF MORE
ACTIVE OPERATION
AUGUST – DECEMBER 1863

I N A LETTER TO MILITARY GOVERNOR ANDREW JOHNSON dated
August 20, 1863, Colonel Hurst estimated the size of his regiment at
849 soldiers with about 300 horses. They were armed with only 186
carbines, "a very great deficiency," he pointed out, "but we have assurance
of getting more horses & Guns soon." His men had decided to spend a
significant portion of their own back payments to purchase Henry repeating
rifles, which could fire forty-five shots per minute.[1] He credited Major
General James Oglesby, commander of the 16th Army Corps Left Wing, for
the present condition of his command having "shown us much kindness
and attention" during their service at Jackson.

Despite his regiment's "unorganized condition" since its inception eleven
months earlier, Hurst boasted it had taken "many Prisoners and had Several
Sharp engagements with Gurrilla [*sic*] bodies infesting West Tenn[essee] and
north Mississippi. [A]ll we ask for now is more Guns and horses and to be
placed in a field of More active operation."[2]

The 6th Tennessee saw more active service on October 7 when it joined
an expedition into north Mississippi led by Colonel LaFayette McCrillis,
commander of the 2nd Cavalry Brigade in the District of Corinth. McCrillis'
intent was to pursue a Confederate force that attacked his command at

---

[1] Memphis *Bulletin*, 31 July 1863. Andrew L. Bresnan, "The Henry Repeating Rife." 17 August
2007. <www.rarewinchesters.com/articles/art_hen01.shtml>
[2] Hurst to Johnson, 20 August 1863. RLB.

Lockhart's Mill two days earlier. The Rebels, after being pursued by the 6th Tennessee, had withdrawn to Salem, Mississippi.[3]

Serving as the advance guard, the 6th Tennessee led the expedition from LaGrange, Tennessee on the morning of October 8 and reached Salem by noon. There they found the enemy "in force" and McCrillis ordered an attack. A battalion under Lieutenant Risden D. Deford of Company H led the initial assault and forced the Confederates to seek cover inside various buildings on the outskirts of town. With the support of the 3rd Illinois Cavalry, the dismounted 6th Tennessee pressed the enemy "west through the town and a mile beyond."

After an hour of skirmishing, McCrillis received word that Confederate reinforcements were advancing from Ripley, Davis' Mill, and Holly Springs, Mississippi. He immediately ordered his command to a more advantageous position atop a long ridge six hundred yards east of Salem. Members of the 6th Tennessee and the 9th Illinois Cavalry under Lieutenant Colonel Jesse J. Phillips were at the front taking the brunt of the rebel attack, which now numbered 4,400 men. Led by Phillips, they managed to take control of the ten to twelve buildings in town at 2:00 p.m. The victory was short-lived, however, as they were quickly forced back by consistent charges upon their flanks.

As the battle progressed through the afternoon, the Union forces' ammunition supply began to dwindle. They had the opportunity to drive the Rebels from town at 2:00 but McCrillis hesitated, fearing that abandoning his position would expose his command to enemy fire when it was "beginning to feel the want of ammunition." The fighting continued into the afternoon as the Union commander awaited much-needed reinforcements. By 5:00 he could wait no longer. Using his last remaining artillery shells as cover, McCrillis ordered his men to withdraw back to LaGrange and left Salem once again in Confederate hands.[4] The only casualties of the 6th Tennessee mentioned by McCrillis were Lieutenant Deford and Major Thomas H. Boswell, who were both seriously but not fatally wounded. Both Colonel Hurst and Major William J. Smith had their horses shot from under them while leading charges during the engagement.[5]

---

[3] O.R. I, 30, part 2: 740.

[4] O.R. I, 30, part 2: 745-747.

[5] *Report of the Adjutant General of the State of Tennessee of the Military Forces of the State from 1861 to 1866* (Nashville: S.C. Mercer, 1866): 475.

The 6th Tennessee returned to north Mississippi three days later with the 7th and 9th Illinois Cavalry and the 7th Kansas Cavalry under Colonel Edward Hatch. The expedition left LaGrange on October 11 and marched back to Salem, where they found the 3rd Michigan already in control of the village. The Rebels had abandoned it and withdrawn toward Holly Springs. Pursuing them the next morning, the expedition encountered their rear guard at Quinn and Jackson's Mill, eight miles south of Collierville, Tennessee and skirmished against them for nine miles.

More formidable opposition was found three miles south of Byhalia, Mississippi under General James R. Chalmers and Colonel Richard V. Richardson. Lieutenant Colonel Jesse J. Phillips of the 9th Illinois Cavalry brought up a howitzer battery to pound the enemy snipers posted in several log cabins in their front. The Confederates advanced but were repulsed by the 7th and 9th Illinois and retreated with the Union expedition still in pursuit until 9:00 that evening.

Under the cover of darkness, the rebels pressed on toward Wyatt, Mississippi where the expedition caught up with them on the morning of October 13. A deep canal surrounded the town and the only bridge across it was in the Confederate rear. The Federals assaulted the town with troops and canister throughout the day, which was answered by charges from its defenders. The fighting continued despite nightfall and a heavy rain as each side bombarded the other with artillery fire. The 6th Tennessee joined the 9th Illinois, 7th Kansas, and the 3rd Michigan under Lieutenant Colonel Phillips in a final charge on Wyatt at 9:00, driving the Rebels "in confusion" across the bridge and out of town.

The next morning, the expedition burned the log houses in the town to prevent the Confederates from using them again. With only twenty-three rounds of ammunition left after two days of consistent fighting and its base of supplies 45 miles north, Colonel Hatch chose to end the pursuit and return to LaGrange. They took with them fifty prisoners, including five commissioned officers and Richardson's adjutant general, as well as two ammunition wagons and 200 arms. Their total losses were forty killed and wounded, with six killed and twenty wounded at Wyatt. The Confederate losses were nine killed and twenty-eight wounded.[6]

---

[6] O.R. I, 30, part 2: 741-742, 762. The Confederate version of the events at Wyatt differs from the Union version. Brigadier General James R. Chalmers claimed that his men endured the Union assault

Another loss to the 6th Tennessee was suffered off the battlefield. Lieutenant Colonel William K.M. Breckenridge died at the Union post in Grand Junction, Tennessee on October 15. The cause of his death was vaguely given as "disease." Colonel Hurst made the necessary adjustments to his command the next day, promoting Major William J. Smith to lieutenant colonel and Captain Orlando H. Shearer of Company I to replace him as major. Adjutant Stanford L. Warren was elevated to captain of Company I and Sergeant Elijah J. Hodges was made adjutant.[7]

In late October Major General Stephen A. Hurlbut, commander of the 16th Army Corps, ordered the 6th Tennessee to operate east of the Mobile and Ohio Railroad in West Tennessee. They were to suppress "with all necessary severity the guerrilla and conscripting parties south of Trenton." He stressed: "[N]o plundering or pillaging by men or officers will be allowed. Colonel Hurst will report weekly through the commanding officer at LaGrange, to the chief of cavalry. The men of this regiment will not be permitted to scatter, but will move in organized force."[8]

When he learned of Hurlbut's plans for the regiment, their former commander, Brigadier General Grenville M. Dodge, suggested that the 6th Tennessee remain at LaGrange instead and prevent the enemy from severing his lines of communication from Corinth, Mississippi to Memphis. Hurlbut agreed but six days later, he received a communication from Brigadier General John D. Stevenson informing him: "Hurst, it seems, abandoned his portion of the road against his express orders from General Dodge. I cannot learn where his command is." The 16th Army Corps commander responded: "Try and find out where Hurst is and get him under your command. Both the Sixth and Seventh Tennessee have behaved badly." He had already ordered the 7th Tennessee under Lt. Col. Issac R.

---

on October 10 despite the downpour that "added greatly to [their] discomfort and rendered many of their guns useless." Nevertheless, he pointed out that they withstood the assault for over three hours before "they withdrew quietly across the river without loss, partially destroying the bridge behind them." Ibid: 762.

[7] Hurst to Johnson, March 4, 1864 in Andrew Johnson Governor Papers 20, Box 1, Folder 4 at TSLA.

[8] O.R. I, 31, part 1: 750-751.

Hawkins to his headquarters in Memphis and promised to "make something of them or break them."[9]

Hurlbut's frustration with the Tennessee Unionists made its way to the desk of Military Governor Andrew Johnson in Nashville. He was confident that more troops could be added to both the 6th and 7th Tennessee but felt a "change in officers" was needed first. He was especially dissatisfied with Hawkins whom he believed to be "entirely incompetent." Hurst, he acknowledged, was "a thoroughly brave man" but he had "no faculty of command or control" over his men "and should be relieved."[10]

Johnson recognized "the incompetency of persons organizing Regiments in this State," but he tolerated them "for the purpose of having their influence in raising troops." He did not think it would be right for Hurlbut to remove Hawkins or Hurst from their commands. They "were among the first in West Tennessee" to begin recruiting Union sympathizers in that part of the state "and after having lost much time, running considerable risk, [and] making considerable Sacrifice," he believed they would be "very harshly treated" if they were "relieved from their commands without their consent."[11]

In need of fresh recruits and supplies, Confederate Major General Nathan Bedford Forrest marched from north Mississippi into Union-occupied West Tennessee in December 1863. He made his headquarters at Jackson and set up recruitment camps in the region. He also rounded up deserters on Confederate rolls and confiscated livestock and other food supplies to feed them all.[12]

Major General Hurlbut was anxious to end Forrest's recruitment activities and began moving forces into position to cut off his escape route back into north Mississippi. With close to 15,000 men, he felt confident in his

---

[9] O.R. I, 31, part 3: 12, 82. Stevenson found the 6th Tennessee that same day. He wrote Hurlbut: "I have sent a special and imperative order to Hurst, who is at Camden, near Purdy [in McNairy County]." Ibid.: 92.

[10] Stephen A. Hurlbut to Andrew Johnson, 18 November 1863. Johnson Papers, Series I, microfilm reel 8 (TSLA).

[11] Johnson to Stephen A. Hurlbut, 29 November 1863 in PAJ 6:496.

[12] Robert Selph Henry, *"First with the Most" Forrest*. New York: Mallard Press, 1991: 204-205.

success. "I think we shall cure Forrest of his ambition to command West Tennessee," he wrote.[13]

On December 23, Forrest and his command—now significantly larger than the 450 men he brought with him a few weeks before and accompanied by a wagon train of supplies—left Jackson and made their way southwest to Estenaula, where they crossed the rain-swollen Hatchie River on the 24th and 25th. While doing so, advance detachments helped clear a path ahead for the main army to eventually push through. After a skirmish at New Castle between Somerville and Bolivar on the morning of the 26th, Forrest baffled his adversaries with a course change. Rather than make his way between LaGrange and Pocahontas as Hurlbut anticipated, he headed west into Somerville instead and eventually crossed the Wolf River near Memphis and back into north Mississippi.[14]

Based on intelligence from his scouts, Hurst erroneously reported to Brigadier General Joseph A. Mower on the 26th that most of Forrest's command was still north of the Hatchie River. He expected Forrest to make his way out in the vicinity of Purdy.[15] According to the memories of Confederate soldier John Hallum, Forrest appeared at Somerville that day to the surprise of Colonel Hurst and his men who were there. Forrest instructed his inexperienced and unarmed recruits to use rifle length sticks as a bluff. The trick worked; according to the story Hurst shouted, "My God, boys! Yonder comes Forrest" and "dug his spurs into his horse's sides in profound realization…[that] 'distance lends enchantment to the view.'" He and his men beat a hasty withdrawal. Hallum continued his fanciful narrative of Hurst's flight:

> His hat was donated to the wind; his long disheveled hair made frantic efforts to fly away; his legs expanded at an angle of forty-five degrees in his heroic efforts to impart celerity to his distressed horse, whose sides were bleeding in sacrifice to glorious war.[16]

---

13 Ibid: 206.
14 Ibid: 208-210. O.R. I, 31, part 3: 500.
15 O.R. I, 31, part 3: 500-501. Mower trusted Hurst "whose opinion I think is highly valuable." Ibid: 500.
16 John Hallum, *Reminiscences of the Civil War.* (Little Rock: Tunnah & Pittard, 1903): 29.

Hallum claimed sixty members of the 6th Tennessee Cavalry were captured and executed at the fairgrounds in Somerville.[17] While not referring to them by name, Forrest reported to Major General Stephen D. Lee that his men fought enemy cavalry at Somerville on the 26th and killed eight to ten men and captured thirty-five.[18] But in a subsequent message to Lieutenant General Leonidas Polk, he referred to the cavalry as the Seventh Illinois Regiment. His men had attacked their rear and "cut them up badly, capturing their wagons, a good many arms and horses, and [capturing] 45 prisoners, and killed and wounded quite a number."[19] Neither report mentioned prisoner executions carried out by his command.

---

[17] Ibid: 29-30. "Sixty of Hurst's men were captured," wrote Hallum, "but the official records put it at thirty-five." He added: "I do not recall any incident of the war related by the general [Forrest] which caused him to overflow with so much laughter as Hurst's flight when the stick brigade was charging on his command." Ibid: 29-30.

[18] O.R. I, 31, part 1: 620.

[19] Ibid: 621.

Col. Fielding Hurst

Lt. Col. William K.M. Breckenridge

Brevet. Brig. Gen. William J. Smith

Cpt. Nathan McDonald Kemp
Company C

Cpt. James L.W. Boatman
Company D

Maj. Daniel M. Emerson

Cpt. William Chandler
Company G

Maj. Stanford L. Warren

Pvt. Pinkney W.H. Lee
Company I

Cpl. James R. Thacker
Company B

Pvt. Wesley Parsons
Company M

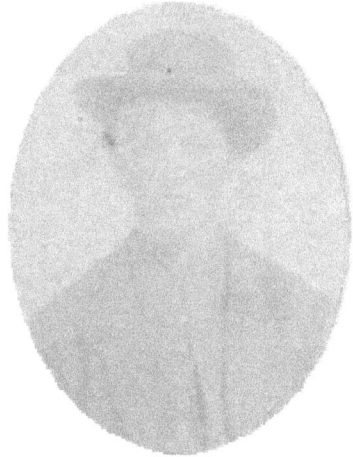

1st Lt. John P. Gibbs
Company L

Military Gov. Andrew Johnson

Gov. William G. Brownlow

Maj. Gen. Benjamin H. Grierson

Maj. Gen. Stephen A. Hurlbut

Lt. Gen. Nathan Bedford Forrest

Brig. Gen. Mason Brayman

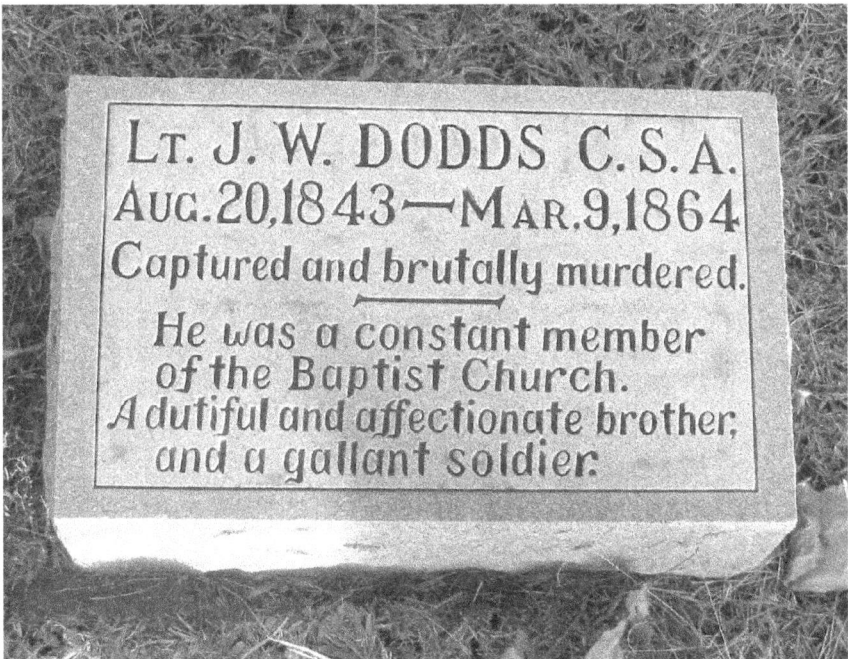

Lt. J. W. DODDS C.S.A.
AUG. 20, 1843 — MAR. 9, 1864
Captured and brutally murdered.
He was a constant member
of the Baptist Church.
A dutiful and affectionate brother,
and a gallant soldier.

Grave of Lt. J. Willis Dodds at Unity Baptist Church
between Middlefork and Jacks Creek, TN

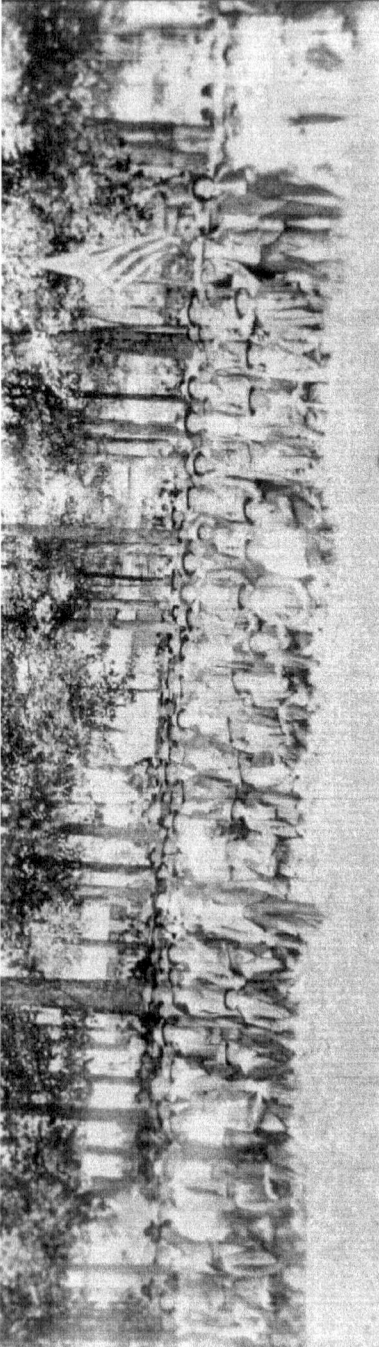

Left: Veterans of the 6th Tennessee Cavalry at a reunion (date unknown). The man in the foreground is believed to be Brevet Brig. Gen. William J. Smith.

Below: Veterans of Company B, 6th Tennessee Cavalry. Soldiers who can be identified are: Miles Plunk (far left, standing) and John Taylor Gage (fifth from right, standing).

Romantic Adventure.

A fanciful depiction of Fielding Hurst (with mustache) and the Purdy, Tennessee pharmacist as Hurst made his escape from Confederate soldiers through the back of his store.

The USS *Tyler* gunboat rescued Fielding Hurst and other Unionist refugees along the Tennessee River in the spring of 1862.

The home of Col. Fielding Hurst
in Purdy, Tennessee (2006)

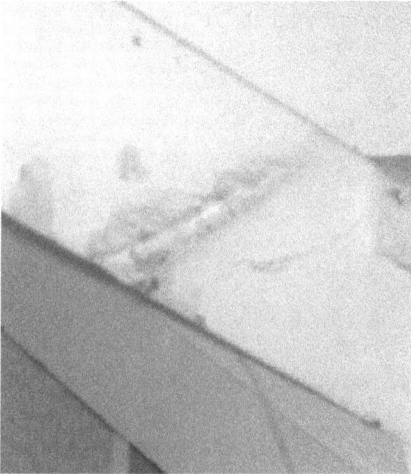

According to legend, someone shot at Col.
Hurst as he fled upstairs. The bullet grazed
the staircase and the mark can still be seen.

Ribbon for Grand Army of the Republic Post No. 7
Adamsville, TN named in honor of Fielding Hurst

State historical marker at Bethel Springs, Tennessee

Above: Tombstone of Col. Fielding Hurst at
Mount Gilead Cemetery, McNairy County TN

Right: Military marker at grave of Col. Hurst
at Mount Gilead Cemetery

GRUB UP
WEST TENNESSEE
JANUARY – FEBRUARY 1864

T HE NEW YEAR BROUGHT TO THE 6TH TENNESSEE CAVALRY new
promise for more active service. Major General William Tecumseh
Sherman was preparing to march through central Mississippi and
destroy rebel supply and transportation facilities at Meridian in what would
be a prelude to his March to the Sea seven months later.[1] He made Brigadier
General William Sooy Smith the new chief of cavalry for the Military
Division of the Mississippi. The 33-year-old former civil engineer arrived in
West Tennessee in mid-January 1864 and began preparing for the cavalry's
role in the campaign to ensure that it would be ready to meet the troublesome rebel cavalry leader, Nathan Bedford Forrest.[2]

Smith discovered he had a lot of work to do. His new command was
missing over two thousand officers and soldiers who were "absent from
duty." A little less than half of those remaining were dismounted for lack of
suitable horses. If he could not find enough horses in the surrounding
countryside, he hoped to secure them from civilians in Memphis as well.
Most of those in service had been poorly maintained, he concluded, and he
reported to Major General Ulysses S. Grant that "a great deal of shoeing"
had been ordered "after their racing about after Forrest" in December. "I

---

[1] Marszalek, *Sherman*: 250-251.
[2] Henry, *Forrest*: 218-219. Hurst, *Forrest*: 147.

will endeavor to secure the same care for all the cavalry commands in our division," he added.[3]

On January 11, 1864, Smith's second-in-command Brigadier General Benjamin H. Grierson ordered Colonel Hurst to establish his regiment's camp at Purdy, Tennessee from which he would "subsist your command upon the country." He was allowed to seize horses in the area with which to mount his command and issue receipts to their owners; the rest were to be sent to the nearest quartermaster.

The order continued:

> Peaceable and loyal citizens will be kindly treated and protected, and your whole energy will be given to the destruction of guerrilla bands that now infest the country. You are particularly warned against allowing your men to straggle from camp or go to their homes. No foraging parties will be sent out except in charge of commissioned officers, who will be held responsible for the actions of the men.

> You will send your tri-monthly and monthly reports as heretofore by special messenger…and will report your whereabouts and progress from time to time…This order is not intended to confine you to any particular locality, but you will move your command in any part of West Tennessee where, in your judgment, it can be used most effectively.[4]

During the first three months of 1864, Smith and Grierson planned to make full use of the regiment in West Tennessee. Colonel Hurst was given greater leeway in his movements than at any point during the war. So confident was Smith in Hurst's ability that he told Major General Grant on January 17: "We have also given Colonel Hurst a roving commission with his regiment…and directed him to 'grub up' West Tennessee. I think he will reduce that district to order."[5] His attitude coincided with the sentiments of Major General Sherman, who after three years of war had come to the realization that if Confederate sympathizers "cannot be made to love us,

---

[3] O.R. I, 32, part 1: 123.
[4] O.R. I, 32, part 1: 66-67.
[5] Ibid: 124.

[they] can be made to fear us, and dread the passage of troops through their country."[6]

Hurst wasted little time realizing the potential of his "roving commission." A few weeks later, the 6th Tennessee disappeared; their whereabouts were unknown even to the military authorities of the 16th Army Corps. Each asked the other, "Have you heard anything of Hurst?" Brigadier General Grierson sent a search party from Memphis on February 5 to find them but its leader had no more success locating them that his superiors.[7]

The 6th Tennessee arrived at Jackson, Tennessee the next day, February 6. A detachment of one hundred cavalrymen rode into town in the afternoon at "full tilt," recalled one citizen, "taking one to all as much by surprise as ever a people was surprised." One of them "caught a glimpse of my horse and before I knew it, he went as a good many others have gone—stolen." They set up camp that evening three miles outside town at the home of one Mr. Bond.[8]

Hurst rode back into town, gathered its prominent residents together, and made his intentions known. He demanded $5,139.25 "in greenbacks or Kentucky funds"—the exact amount taken from his command as the result of Mrs. A.A. Newman's vandalism complaint six months earlier. If it was not given to him, he threatened to burn the town. The fact that Mrs. Newman, the focus of their threat, was no longer a resident of Jackson made no difference. Twenty citizens promised to pay the ransom, but they asked for five days to raise it. Hurst agreed and went with his command to camp on the property of Bob Chester two miles outside town.[9]

Five days later, Hurst returned and was given the ransom. After dining in Jackson, he and his men returned to the Chester home in the company of "women and children." The next day, a slave seen talking with a member of the 6th Tennessee was shot and his body tossed into the Forked Deer River.

---

[6] Burke Davis, *Sherman's March* (New York: Vintage Books, 1988): 17.
[7] O.R. I, 32, part 3: 331, 332, 343.
[8] Williams, *Historic Madison*: 179.
[9] Mary Chester to William Butler Chester, February 8, 1864.

Those who murdered him thought he was an informant for the Union regiment.[10]

The 6th Tennessee traveled southwest to Brownsville on February 14. Hurst "appeared to be angry" after learning there might be Confederate soldiers hiding in town and "ordered the Town to be burned," recalled one resident. His men knocked down the doors of local homes searching for them. Thirty or forty soldiers asked to be let inside a dry goods store that was closed for the Sabbath. The weather was cold and rainy and they asked the owners how much their overcoats were. When told the price, the soldiers said it was too expensive and took the overcoats along with hats, shoes, coffee, sugar, and woolen cloth without paying or giving vouchers to reimburse the owners.[11]

That night several homes and businesses on the south and east side of the court square were set on fire.[12] Attorney Edward J. Read charged the regiment not only with burned ones owned by Confederate sympathizers but three businesses owned by three of "the best Union men about Brownsville" as well. "Is that any way for him or any Federal officer to do?" he asked Andrew Johnson on March 19. These and other Unionists had left town and sought refuge in Illinois. "It appears that old Satan had been turned loose to go about and [is] injuring the innocent," Read lamented.[13]

Despite its residents paying a ransom to prevent it, Hurst and his command returned to Jackson on February 25 and set fire to buildings on the southeast corner of Lafayette and Market Streets. Fourteen structures were consumed before the blazes were finally extinguished. Many could have been saved if those fighting the fires had full use of the town well; the ropes had been intentionally cut.[14]

Not every member of the 6th Tennessee Cavalry approved of Hurst's total war tactics. Captain James L.W. Boatman of Company D believed burning homes and harassing wives and children of Confederate soldiers

---

[10] Williams, *Historic Madison*: 179.

[11] Southern Claims Commission No. 1507 Petition of Williams Simms and L.Y. Bledsoe. <www.footnote.com> The owners applied for reimbursement for their losses estimated at $1,691.25. But the Southern Claims Commission ruled it was "an instance of lawless plunder and depredation" and disallowed the claim. Ibid.

[12] Ibid.

[13] Edward J. Read to Andrew Johnson, 19 March 1864 in PAJ 6: 648.

[14] Williams, *Historic Madison*: 179-180. Williams noted that Jackson "from Lafayette to Baltimore [Streets] and from Shannon to Market [Streets] had been burned by Hurst's men." Ibid: 190.

were unnecessary acts of war. According to family tradition when he learned of plans to burn a particular home, he would warn the family ahead of time and even help them hide their valuables and find a safe place to hide.[15]

Although the leaders of the 16th Army Corps were oblivious to the activities of the 6th Tennessee Cavalry, there was one man who was very aware. "Hurst is still reported in West Tennessee," Major General Nathan Bedford Forrest wrote from his headquarters at Columbus, Kentucky on March 10, "and a portion of Jackson and Brownsville have been burned by his men."[16] There were also reports of brutal murders committed against Confederate soldiers under Forrest's command. He assigned Lieutenant Colonel William M. Reed to investigate the arsons and murders in West Tennessee.

A few weeks later, Forrest received the results of the investigation and sent a copy to Lieutenant General Leonidas Polk, asking that it be "sent to some newspaper for publication. Such conduct should be known to the world."[17] A copy was also forwarded to the 16th Army Corps commanders at Memphis on March 22. In it, Forrest wrote:

> It appears that within the past two months, seven cases of deliberate murder have been committed in this department, most of them and all believed to have been perpetrated by the command of Colonel Hurst. I therefore demand the surrender of Col. Fielding Hurst and the officers and men of his command guilty of these murders, to be dealt with by the C.S. authorities as their offenses require.

The report included accounts of the murders of six Forrest cavalrymen and one civilian attributed to members of the 6th Tennessee. Three soldiers from John F. Newsom's regiment had been captured in McNairy County on February 15 and their bodies found three days later in Haywood County. A

---

15 Reflections Committee, *Reflections*: 303.
16 O.R. I, 32, part 3: 609.
17 O.R. I, 32, part 3: 663.

"deformed and almost helpless" 16-year-old McNairy County boy had been arrested and killed. A Private Martin of Wilson's regiment had been murdered and denied burial for the four-day period that the regiment was in the area.

The most horrible crime was the murder of Lieutenant Willis Dodds of Newsom's regiment. He had been arrested at his father's Henderson County home and brutally tortured by his captors. An eyewitness who saw his body told Reed that Dodds had been "most horribly mutilated, the face having been skinned, the nose cut off, and the body otherwise barbarously lacerated and most wantonly injured, and that his death was brought about by the most inhumane process of torture."[18]

Forrest's diatribe against Hurst and his officers and his demand for their surrender also contained a more ominous threat:

> Whereas it has come to the knowledge of the major-general commanding that Col. Fielding Hurst, commanding [the 6th] Regiment U.S. [Tennessee Cavalry] Volunteers, has been guilty of wanton extortion upon the citizens of Jackson, Tenn., and other places, guilty of depredations upon private property, guilty of house burning, guilty of murders, both of citizens and soldiers of the Confederate States; and whereas demand had been duly made upon the military authorities of the United States for the surrender of said Col. Fielding Hurst and such officers and men of his command as are guilty of these outrages; and whereas this just demand has been refused by said authorities; I therefore declare the aforesaid Fielding Hurst, and the officers and men of his command, outlaws, and not entitled to be treated as prisoners of war falling into the hands of the forces of the Confederate States.[19]

Hurst responded to Forrest's charges with accusations of his own that attributed equally brutal murders of Unionists in West Tennessee to soldiers under Forrest's command. He pointed out to Brigadier General Grierson the murders of four civilians "in cold blood [and] without the slightest provocation."

---

[18] O.R. I, 32, part 3: 117-119.
[19] O.R. I, 32, part 3: 119.

> These victims of this murderous band were the friends and rela-
> tives of the families of soldiers now in the U.S. service, who were
> at home endeavoring, by labor and economy, to make a support
> for and, to some extent, alleviate the distressed condition of the
> wives and children, widows and orphans, of Union soldiers...I
> have presented these cases as mere specimens of the various out-
> rages to which loyal men and their wives and children are daily
> subject.

One elderly Gibson County Unionist whose two sons were members of the 6th Tennessee had been kidnapped and his captors demanded $200 from his family to release him. His distraught wife paid the ransom only to be told that they would kill him anyway. Three days later his body was found near his home, "dead and horribly mangled."

Among the victims was Hurst's own nephew William Hurst (son of his brother Elza), who was tied him to a tree and shot between the eyes. William's mother had also been injured when they tried to steal her bed sheets from under her, causing her to fall to the floor and break her hip. A Hurst family story claimed the men were looking for Elza Hurst, believing he had stolen horses from them. His wife claimed he was out of state to explain his absence. The men saw his son plowing in a nearby field, dragged him to the road, and killed him instead.[20]

Hurst responded directly to Forrest's accusations. "I love my country and am too proud of her flag to ever disgrace it by that mode of warfare that Tennesseans must and will adopt if such outrages are not suppressed," he asserted.[21]

The matter resurfaced in late June 1864 when Forrest exchanged letters with 16th Army Corps commander Major General Cadwallader C. Washburn concerning his assault on Fort Pillow the previous month.

---

[20] Virginia Branch, *The Hurst Nation, A Family History*: 10. William Roark, Roland D. Williams, and David Spencer were indicted by the McNairy County Grand Jury for the murder of William Hurst that took place on April 1, 1864. McNairy County Circuit Court Minutes, Book B: 7.

[21] O.R. I, 39, part 2: 56. The four civilians mentioned by Hurst were B.A. Crawford and William Bowlin of Weakley County and John Calaway Huddleston and William Hurst of McNairy County. Huddleston was Hurst's brother-in-law, the husband of his sister Emily Lauretta. Family tradition says his horse returned home with only an empty saddle. He was never seen again. Judy Malone to the author, January 29, 1995. William Hurst was his nephew and the son of his brother Elza.

Commenting on the death of the fort's commander, Major Lionel Bradford, during an escape attempt after his capture, Forrest wrote:

> If he was improperly killed nothing would afford me more pleasure than to punish the perpetrators to the full extent of the law, and to show you how I regard such transactions I can refer you to my demand upon Major-General Hurlbut (no doubt upon file in your office) for the delivery to Confederate authorities of one Col. Fielding Hurst and others of his regiment, who deliberately took out and killed 7 Confederate soldiers, one of whom they left to die after cutting off his tongue, punching out his eyes, splitting his mouth on each side to the ears, and cutting off his privates.[22]

Washburn replied to Forrest that Hurst "indignantly denies the charge against him." The Union officer asked Forrest for specific names and localities related to the murders. Should the accusations prove to be true, "you may rest assured that I shall use every effort in my power to have the parties accused tried, and, if found guilty, properly punished."[23]

---

[22] O.R. I, 32, part 1: 592.
[23] Ibid: 602.

RUN LIKE SO
MANY DEVILS
MARCH 1864

O N MARCH 22, 1864, Brigadier General Benjamin Grierson ordered
Fielding Hurst to prepare his regiment "for an immediate and
active campaign in West Tennessee." Forrest was in the region
conscripting civilians and deserters to replenish his command and the 16th
Army Corps wanted his movements closely observed. "You will go with no
transportation," instructed Grierson, "and only with such rations &c as the
men can carry. Take a full supply of ammunition...Come in [to Memphis] on
[the] first train and report for further instructions."[1] Grierson telegraphed
Major General William T. Sherman of his decision the next day, telling him
that "the old cavalry" was on furlough and he hesitated to use the infantry.
He resolved instead to send the 6th Tennessee with 800 to 1,000 men "to
hang upon, harass, and watch the movements of the enemy. [They] will start
tomorrow via Somerville and Bolivar or Estenaula."[2]

Grierson sent word to Hurst on the 24th that Forrest "with a considerable force of cavalry" was at Jackson "with the intention," he believed, "of
either crossing the Tennessee [River] and operating in the rear of Chattanooga or of striking some point on the Mississippi or Ohio Rivers." He
ordered him "to move with the effective force of your command...without
train or other incumbrance [sic]...via Somerville toward Jackson, crossing the
Hatchie River at Estenaula or such other point as the information you

---

[1] O.R. I, 32, part 3: 116.
[2] O.R. I, 32, part 3: 132.

obtain may justify." With the "outlaw" declaration placed on them by Forrest in mind, Grierson stressed:

> The object of your expedition is to hang upon and harass the enemy with a view of impending his movements as much as possible. You will not bring him into a general engagement, but rather cut off and capture his foraging parties, stragglers, &c.
>
> Hold your command well in hand, and do not allow yourself to be drawn into any trap or to be surprised.
>
> Take any forage or provisions you may find which may be necessary to subsist your command.
>
> Extend protection as far as possible to people of known loyalty, and rather forage upon secession sympathizers. You are particularly cautioned against allowing your men to straggle or pillage. Issue and enforce the strictest orders upon this subject, as a deviation from this rule may prove fatal to yourself and command.
>
> Look well with reliable scouts to your flanks and rear, as a portion of the enemy's force is at present south, and will endeavor to form a junction with Forrest.
>
> Communicate as often as possible by courier or otherwise with the nearest Federal forces, and follow the enemy as long as you may consider it safe and expedient.
>
> With your excellent knowledge of the country, I rely upon your ability to inflict serious injury upon the enemy without much loss to your command.[3]

The 6th Tennessee marched from the vicinity of Memphis on the morning of March 25 and proceeded toward Somerville and Bolivar. At this time, Assistant Adjutant General S.L. Woodward ordered Colonel George W. Waring Jr. to send 300 soldiers from his command to operate on the regiment's left flank. Major Robert M. Thompson left Raleigh with units of the 6th Tennessee under his command to rendezvous with Hurst north of Somerville.[4]

---

[3] O.R. I, 32, part 3: 145-146.
[4] O.R. I, 32, part 3: 169.

Three days later Confederate Colonel James J. Neely, commanding a brigade of Forrest's cavalry, rode into Bolivar from northern Mississippi on his way to join Forrest at Jackson some 27 miles away. Their appearance was rather unexpected by the town's citizens, recalled one resident, "a hungry & destitute crowd seldom [to] come upon a poverty Stricken community." This was the Rebel force Brigadier General Grierson had warned Hurst about before he left Memphis.[5]

Shortly after his arrival at Bolivar, Neely learned that the 6th Tennessee was approaching town from nearby Whiteville. He positioned his men in and around an abandoned Union dirt fort one and a half miles west of Bolivar. When the regiment did not show, he ordered his command to camp there for the night and continue its march to Jackson the next morning.[6]

Scouts from the 6th Tennessee discovered Neely's brigade on the evening of March 28, estimating its strength at about 800 men. Despite being outnumbered, Hurst decided to attack the Rebels the next morning. He disregarded Brigadier General Grierson's explicit order not to become involved in "a general engagement."[7]

On the morning of March 29, Colonel Neely assembled his command and began marching toward Jackson. A courier caught up with him and told him the Union regiment was indeed approaching the western outskirts of Bolivar. Neely quickly ordered his men back to their former position at the redoubt, positioning the 12th and 15th Tennessee in and around it while the dismounted 14th Tennessee acted as skirmishers. The advantage was theirs as the redoubt occupied a hill overlooking the 6th Tennessee's approach on the Whiteville Road.

The sky was clear, the weather cool and "very windy" as the 6th Tennessee Cavalry reached the edge of town and approached the dirt fort. At about 9:00 a.m. the 14th Tennessee charged through the woods toward them. The Confederates "must have had some whiskey," remembered one observer, "for Col[onel] Hurst's command rode up and the Confederates gave a yell fired their guns and charged, [and] Hurst's men wheeled and ran." Private

---

[5] John Houston Bills Diary, 28 March 1864 entry. Microfilm 1 at TSLA. Neely reached Bolivar at about 9:00 a.m. Ibid.

[6] William T. Alderson, ed. "The Civil War Reminiscences of John Johnston." *Tennessee Historical Quarterly*, 13.3 (September 1954): 272.

[7] Henry M. Lawrence to Dr. C. Revis, 5 April 1864. Account 68-267 in Manuscript Division at TSLA.

Alexander Young of Company M described it as "A Stampeed Rite at the Start," the regiment having "to Reetreat [*sic*] in disorder."[8]

"As soon as our horses could be brought up," recalled Confederate private John Johnston, "we with the other [mounted] men who came up, pressed after [them] on horseback, and the affair now became more like hunters on a chase than a battle." The 6th Tennessee regrouped and formed a line of battle along a hilltop above Little Clear Run Creek. This proved to be an excellent vantage point as their pursuers had to cross a bridge and ride across a valley to get to them, thus exposing the Confederates to their fire. The enemy pressed toward the bridge but they were "badly scattered and without a semblance of order." Had the 6th Tennessee held its position and fired upon the bridge and its approach, Johnston admitted, the Confederate advance could have been restrained.

Instead, the 6th Tennessee continued its flight toward Whiteville and the Confederates stayed in pursuit. A final stand was made outside a wooded area, but the regiment had no idea how many Rebels were hiding inside. "After a few shots from our skirmishers," continued Johnston, "they broke ranks and scampered away again. We did not pursue them further. We had an exciting chase for about 14 or 15 miles and were willing to stop." Their flight continued until the regiment reached the safety of Memphis.[9]

The "chase" proved costly both in casualties and to the reputation of the 6th Tennessee Cavalry. The Confederate reports estimated their losses as thirty-five killed and thirty captured as well as a guidon[10] and their entire wagon train consisting of two ambulances and five wagons. Inside the wagons were the regimental records and 50,000 rounds of ammunition. The records revealed that the regiment had 650 men in the engagement. Colonel Neely's superior, Brigadier General James R. Chalmers, boasted in his report: "Colonel Neely, of the Thirteenth Tennessee, met the traitor Hurst at Bolivar, and after a short conflict... drove Hurst hatless into Memphis, leaving in our hands all his wagons, ambulances, papers, and his mistresses, both black and white."[11]

---

[8] Alderson, *Reminiscences*: 272-273. Bills Diary, March 29, 1864. Robinson Civil War Questionnaire: 16.
[9] Alderson, *Reminiscences*: 273-275.
[10] A guidon was a small flag that designated a particular military unit.
[11] O.R. I, 32, part 3: 733. O.R. I, 32, part 1: 608, 620, 623. Thomas Jordan and J.P. Pryor, *The Campaigns of Lieut.-Gen. N.B. Forrest and of Forrest's Cavalry* (Dayton, OH: Press of Morningside Bookshop, 1973): 419. This is the third recorded instance in which Hurst allegedly brought women with him on military expeditions.

The Union version of the engagement was no less blunt. Major P. Jones Yorke of the 1st Cavalry Brigade reported that the regiment "was attacked and whipped...by a brigade of the enemy's cavalry."[12] Among the casualties were Captain John W. Moore of Company L, 2nd Lieutenant Hugh L. Neely, and Corporal Thomas Ezell of Company M. Captain William Carroll Holt of Company M was captured and sent to several Confederate prison camps, including Andersonville, Georgia. He eventually escaped and made his way back home "over the mountains, through snow & sleet, without sufficient clothing to Keep from suffering with cold, & no money to buy more."[13]

Writing to family and friends, soldiers from the 6th Tennessee tried to rationalize their actions during the battle. "Let me say to you [this] is the first time...[we] ever had to run," explained Private Henry M. Lawrence of Company I on April 5. "[W]e retreated 14 miles and the daring devils firing on the rear all the Time[.] [W]e would...fight awhile and then run to Keep them from flanking us." Some claimed they were outnumbered worse than their scouts had led them to believe and that Neely had been reinforced overnight.[14]

The surrender of Union City, Tennessee by Colonel Issac R. Hawkins of the 7th Tennessee (U.S.) Cavalry on March 24 to Colonel W.L. Duckworth's detachment of Forrest's cavalry was foremost on the mind of Private Lawrence during the chase. He had heard of their "baseful surrender," a course of action that might have been acceptable to the 7th Tennessee, he wrote, "but Col. Hurst would have Spent his last drop of Blood" rather than give up. Instead, they "would run like so many devils when overpowered," a much better strategy he reasoned "than giving up...and having a fort to fight In."

A few soldiers claimed Colonel Neely sent a flag of truce to the 6th Tennessee and demanded their surrender. Lawrence wrote his friends in Weakley County, Tennessee that Hurst's response was for Neely "to get us by fighting if [he] could, but no other way." He claimed the 6th Tennessee "had done more [fighting] than any other Reg[iment] in the service."

---

12 O.R. I, 32, part 1: 585.

13 Lawrence to Revis, 5 April 1864. William Carroll Holt Military Pension Application at National Archives (Washington D.C.).

14 Lawrence to Revis, 5 April 1864. "[T]his is the first time the whole command ever had to run & in short when we found our strength too weak we made good time in running for 14 Long miles and then Lost only 25 or 30 men." Lawrence to William Lawrence and family, April 5, 1864.

Surrendering to a brigade of Forrest's cavalry meant certain retaliation for the murders the Confederate cavalry leader claimed they had committed.[15]

Private Lawrence claimed Neely's demand for surrender came with the threat of "no quarter" if it were not done.

> Forrest said no Quarters...well we have 40 of their men in our [hands] & by god no Quarters to them (Lex Taliones[16]) we never have mistreated any Reg[ular] Southern soldier nor will we yet if they will respect us as soldiers when taken prisoners if not Eye for Eye & Tooth for Tooth.[17]

The soldiers of the 6th Tennessee confessed to their families and friends that their defeat at Bolivar "was an awful stampede" made worse by having no reinforcements closer than forty miles. The regiment was "Badly whiped [*sic*]," wrote Private James Denham of Company L. Yet Private Lawrence remained optimistic; he encouraged "the young men" in his hometown of Dresden, Tennessee "to delay no Longer but fall into ranks if with no others but the 6th Tenn[essee]."[18]

---

[15] Lawrence to Revis, 5 April 1864. Jack Young to "Brother," April 8, 1864. Account 68-267 in Manuscript Division at TSLA.

[16] *Lex talionis* is the Law of Retaliation in which the punishment matches the crime committed.

[17] Lawrence to Revis, 5 April 1864.

[18] Ibid. James Denham to J.F. Denham, 7 April 1864. Account 68-267 in Manuscript Division at TSLA. William B. Little Military Pension Application at National Archives (Washington D.C.).

DISMOUNTED AND UNASSIGNED

APRIL 1864 – JUNE 1865

THE HUMILIATING DEFEAT AT BOLIVAR marked the regiment's sparing use thereafter by the 16th Army Corps commanders. Colonel Hurst's actions were scrutinized, particularly his decision—against the orders of Brigadier General Greirson—to take with him five supply wagons containing 50,000 rounds of ammunition, abandon them during the flight, and allow them to be captured by the enemy. Hurst was placed under a general court-martial at Memphis from April 11 to April 30. Although no charges resulted from the investigation, subsequent assignments given to him reflected a lack of confidence in his competence and leadership.[1]

During Hurst's absence, Grierson ordered the transferal of 200 soldiers from the regiment to the District of Eastern Arkansas for temporary duty at Helena. Four companies led by Lieutenant Francis Tucker consisting of 177 men remained until June 12. Their commanding officer, Brigadier General N.B. Buford, remarked that they were a "raw" and "undisciplined" unit.[2]

Another detachment with soldiers from Company E was stationed at Fort Pillow on the Tennessee River when Nathan Bedford Forrest led his controversial assault on April 12, 1864. The garrison's defenders were Tennessee Unionists and African-American soldiers. Local residents called it

---

[1] Gary R. Blankenship, *Fielding Hurst, Tennessee Tory: A Study of a West Tennessee Unionist of the American Civil War* (Master's Thesis, Memphis State University, Gary R. Blankenship, 1977): 99.
[2] O.R. I, 32, part 3: 350. TICW: 335.

"a nest of outlaws" that harassed them and pillaged on their farms. The Northern press depicted the battle as a "massacre" as sixty-six percent of the black soldiers and thirty-five percent of the Unionists were killed in the 580-man garrison. Lieutenant and Adjutant Mack J. Leaming of the 13th Tennessee (Union) Cavalry was spared a similar fate when a Confederate soldier, ready to kill him, discovered he was a Mason. Though seriously wounded, Leaming survived and was reassigned to the 6th Tennessee with a promotion to major. Thirteen members of Company E were captured but none killed.[3]

Nathan Bedford Forrest boasted of his success to Confederate president Jefferson Davis:

> I am gratified in being able to say that the capture of [Issac R.] Hawkins at Union City, and [Major William F.] Bradford at Fort Pillow, with the recent defeat...of Colonel Hurst, has broken up the Tennessee Federal regiments in [this] country. Their acts of oppression, murder, and plunder made them a terror to the whole land. For murders committed I demanded that Fielding Hurst be dealt with as their offenses required...Hurst and his command have, as I learn, been sent, in consequence of this demand, to some other locality.[4]

Forrest's assumption that Hurst's command had left the region, much less as the result of his surrender demand, was premature. Not that the embattled colonel would not have welcomed a transfer elsewhere. Hurst was unhappy with his regiment's limited duties and had renewed his efforts to be stationed closer to the Tennessee River and his soldiers' families. He sent a letter with Major Robert M. Thompson, who was traveling to Nashville to meet with Military Governor Andrew Johnson, in late April. Hurst wrote Johnson:

> West Tennessee has furnished a number of men for the United States Service, who entered the Service for the purpose of defending their homes from the invasions of the enemy; and yet these men are compelled to Stay here [in Memphis] and at other points remote from their homes, while the rebels are allowed to

---

[3] RAJ: 456. Jack Hurst, *Nathan Bedford Forrest, A Biography* (New York: Alfred A. Knopf, 1993): 173-174.
[4] O.R. I, 32, part 1: 612.

float at large, sacking, and plundering, their families of all they
have to Subsist upon...Now, what I desire, is to be Stationed at
Some point on the Tennessee River, above Fort Henry, where I
can be of Some Service to the families of the men in my Regiment. I know I cannot go there now, but I do not think the time
is far distant when I can, and I therefore earnestly request you, to
use your influence to that effect and if possible have us ordered
there.[5]

No longer was the 6th Tennessee looked upon by their Northern
superiors and fellow soldiers as a valuable asset; now they "frequently taunt
us with being 'Conquered Rebels' and insinuate that they had just as well
have us on the other Side as not," wrote Hurst. "This does not at all Suit
me," he continued:

I don't like to be compelled to Keep my Regiment where a Rebel
has more influence over the authorities that a loyal man, neither
do I like the idea of guarding Rebel Property, whilst the owners
of said Property are living luxuriantly under the protection of my
Government, and at the Same Time plotting against that Government [or being] under the immediate command of men who
have 'Cotton on the brain' to Such an extent as to Cause them to
neglect their duty to the Government.[6]

In early June, the soldiers of the 6th Tennessee were ordered to dismount
and give their horses to the 4th Missouri, 19th Pennsylvania, and the 2nd
New Jersey Cavalry in their brigade. With no action forthcoming from
Andrew Johnson, Hurst directed his frustration and determination to be
transferred toward the state's adjutant general, Brigadier General Alvin C.
Gillem. Now he wanted completely out of West Tennessee and away from
the control of the 16th Army Corps. He wrote Gillem on June 29:

From the beginning of the organization of this Reg[imen]t, im-
pediments and bearriers [sic] of evry [sic] conceivable Shape have
been thrown in our way by those, who ought to have been our
friends, [namely] the Military Authorities of the 16" Army Corps.

---

[5] Hurst to Johnson, 29 April 1864 in Andrew Johnson Military Governor Papers, Box 1, Folder 4,
Account 124 at TSLA.
[6] Ibid. Hurst's reference to "Cotton [sic] on the brain" refers to illegal cotton trading conducted by
Union officers and U.S. Treasury agents. By June 1864, prices rose to $1 a pound and ended the
illegal trading. PAJ 6:687fn.

No favors have been Shown us, and no encouragement what[so]ever has been extended towards us, all the Success we had being attributable alone to the genuine patriotism and Self Sacrifice of the Officers and men who compose the Reg[imen]t...[W]e are placed here [e]xclusively under Yankee Officers, who have no Sympathy, for a loyal Tennessean and being anxious to further the cause of the Government and crush this Rebellion as Speedily as possible. I would most respectfully and earnestly ask to be removed to the department of the Cumberland [in Middle Tennessee] where I will be under the Controll [*sic*], if not of a Tennessean, of at least men who believe, that there is some patriotism South of the Ohio River.[7]

In July, Brigadier General Edward Hatch launched an investigation into the extortion by Hurst against the citizens of Jackson, Tennessee five months earlier. He reported to Major General Cadwallader C. Washburn that Hurst claimed the money was taken to compensate his men for the amount deducted from their regimental payroll. But Hurst confessed that the funds had not been shared with his men nor had he turned them over to his superior officers. The ransom had instead been deposited with a Memphis dry goods business called Pitser Miller and Company "for his own private benefit."[8] Hatch demanded that Hurst be arrested and Pitser Miller and Company ordered to turn the funds over the military authorities. "Undoubtedly there are many unauthorized robberies of this kind of which Col. Hurst is guilty," he reported. "I have been told by Col. Hurst himself of money to large amounts which have been obtained from sources of this kind."[9]

---

[7] Hurst to Alvin C. Gillem, 29 June 1864. Tennessee State Adjutant General Records in Manuscript Division at TSLA.
[8] Edward Hatch to Cadwallader C. Washburn, 24 July 1864. Hurst Military Records at TSLA. P. Miller and Company was owned by Pitser Miller and Thomas R. Smith and located on 276 Second Street in Memphis, Tennessee. T.M. Halpin, ed. *Memphis City Directory 1866* (Memphis, TN: Bingham, Williams & Company, 1866): 153.
[9] Hatch to Washburn, July 24, 1864. Hurst Military Records.

Ten months later, Hatch learned that William Chandler, former captain of Company G (who was married to one of Hurst's nieces) had committed similar acts of extortion against residents of McNairy County totaling $50,000. "Hurst has already taken about $100,000 out of West Tennessee in blackmail when [he was] colonel of the Sixth [Tennessee] Cavalry," he added.[10]

It is not known if Colonel Hurst was ever punishment as a result of the investigation. But the pleas he made for reassignment elsewhere still fell on deaf ears. As late as August 31, his command was still in West Tennessee and attached to the 16th Army Corps, dismounted and unassigned. On October 5, four companies were sent to Shoal Creek in northern Alabama for temporary duty under Brigadier General James D. Morgan.[11]

It was not until the fall of 1864 that the 6th Tennessee Cavalry was finally transferred outside West Tennessee. On October 24 it was reassigned to the command of Major General James H. Wilson at Nashville and placed in the 2nd Brigade of the 7th Cavalry Division under Brigadier General Joseph F. Knife. The regiment served limited duty during the Battle of Nashville December 15 and 16 but suffered no casualties. The muster roll for Company I indicated that it took part in the pursuit of Confederate General John Bell Hood and the defeated Army of Tennessee as far south as Spring Hill. The detachment returned to Nashville "Wet Cold Hungry and Tired" on December 21.[12]

Five days before the Battle of Nashville, Colonel Fielding Hurst submitted his resignation as commander of the 6th Tennessee Cavalry. At fifty-three years old, he was in bad health and suffering from scurvy, an ailment he contracted during his imprisonment in the winter of 1861-1862. His resignation became effective on January 8, 1865.[13]

---

[10] O.R. I, 49, part 2: 751. Hatch thought Chandler was Hurst's brother-in-law, but Chandler had actually married Hurst's niece, Narcissa Moore.

[11] TICW: 336.

[12] Blankenship, "Hurst": 85. Company I Muster Roll for November-December 1864. National Archives (Washington D.C.).

[13] Hurst Military Records.

Leadership of the regiment passed to his second-in-command, Lieutenant Colonel William J. Smith. Born in Birmingham, England on September 24, 1823, Smith immigrated to the United States at an early age and worked as a painter at Goshen, New York before moving south in 1846. He was a veteran of the Mexican War having served as a private in Wheat's company of Tennessee volunteers.

When Union troops occupied Grand Junction, Tennessee, Smith raised the "Stars and Stripes" over his cotton plantation and aided the 4th Illinois Cavalry as a scout and a worker repairing the Mississippi Central Railroad between Grand Junction and Bolivar. When the Union army left, his secessionist neighbors raided his plantation and burned his cotton bales, forcing him to seek the protection of military service. On September 18, 1862 he enlisted in the 6th Tennessee as a private, but his prior military experience helped elevate him through the ranks as quartermaster, major, lieutenant colonel, and finally colonel.[14]

On December 10, 1864, the 6th Tennessee was reassigned to the 4th Division in the Cavalry Corps of the Military Division of the Mississippi under the command of Brevet Major General Emory Upton. It was transferred less than a month later to the 1st Brigade of the 6th Division under Brigadier General Richard W. Johnson. The regiment remained at Edgefield, east of Nashville, until March 1865.

At this time, Lieutenant Colonel Smith was charged with "Conduct unbecoming an Officer and a Gentleman" for ordering 2nd Lieutenant James A. Magnum of Company M tied to a tree for five to six hours "in cold and disagreeable winter weather" on the afternoon and early evening of January 17, 1865. He was being punished for an unspecified offense. The crime may have been drunkenness, a personal vice that surfaced again a month later. Smith declared Mangrum "totally unfit for the position he holds" and recommended that he be dismissed from the service, which was done on June 2.[15]

---

[14] William J. Smith Military Records at National Archives (Washington D.C.). "Gen. W.J. Smith Falls Dead on the Street." Memphis *Commercial-Appeal*, 30 November 1913.
[15] Smith Military Records. William J. Smith to W.D. Whipple, 8 February 1865 in RLB.

In April 1865, the 6th Tennessee was stationed at Pulaski in south-central Middle Tennessee where its primary responsibility was to guard government cattle. Their encampment was situated in a muddy, unhealthy area, a point that was brought up by Major W.B. Smith of the 8th Michigan Cavalry to Brigadier General Richard W. Johnson. They are "in a fine state of discipline and organization," Smith noted on April 28, but they were "sadly wanting in Camp equipage." Their arms and clothing were dirty due to the poor camp conditions. "A change of Camp is indispensable," he recommended, "to the welfare of the Reg[imen]t." By late June, they had been relocated to a more satisfactory location.[16]

Johnson did not limit the regiment's duties to simply guarding cattle. On May 21, he ordered Captain Risden D. Deford of Company H to pursue several guerrilla bands that were terrorizing the Shoal Creek area in Giles County, Tennessee and Lauderdale County, Alabama. He was warned to "use the greatest diligence and vigilance to restrain his men from the pillage of peaceable citizens or from revenging any supposed wrongs or grudges."[17] The assignment lasted two months and sent them as far south as Florence, Alabama, where Deford allegedly hanged thirty guerrillas in the street.[18]

A native of Allegheny City, Pennsylvania, Captain Deford moved south with his parents to Lauderdale County before the war began. His father was a Methodist preacher and Deford often accompanied him on his circuit, giving him knowledge of the area he would use during the war. His family opposed slavery and this stance created tensions between Reverend Deford and his Southern congregations. Three secessionists attacked the younger Deford on a Florence street. They were prepared to stone him to death when a secessionist bystander intervened and saved his life. In May 1863, he was assigned as a guide for Colonel Florence M. Cornyn in a Union expedition through northern Alabama and identified the homes of Confederate sympathizers. Deford intentionally passed by the home of the man who had saved his life.[19]

---

[16] W.B. Smith to Richard W. Johnson, 28 April 1865 in RLB. Harvey Knotts to L.E. Knotts, 29 June 1865 in Account 68-287 in Manuscript Division at TSLA. John W. Plunk Military Records at National Archives (Washington D.C.).

[17] O.R. I, 49, part 2: 893.

[18] Wade Pruitt, *Bugger Saga: The Civil War Story of Guerrilla and Bushwhacker Warfare in Lauderdale County, Alabama and Southern Middle Tennessee* (Columbia, TN: P-Vine Press, 1977): 57.

[19] Andrew P. Hitt, *Short Life Sketches of Some Prominent Hardin Countians* (Savannah, TN: Custom Productions, n.d.): 31. Pruitt, *Bugger Saga*: 23, 57-58, 81-82.

The 6th Tennessee Cavalry was discharged from military service at Pulaski, Tennessee on July 26, 1865 two months after General Edmund Kirby Smith surrendered the last remaining Confederate armies west of the Mississippi River. The regiment's veterans made their way, many on foot, to receive their last payments at Nashville before returning to their homes.[20] Some had a more pleasant journey than others. "I walk[ed] from Nashville home [and] Had all the good Whiskey I wanted," recalled Private William M. Parker of Company M.[21]

Three members of the regiment had a more eventful and unfortunate journey home that almost claimed their lives. Private Olynthus G. Shelton and Corporal Morgan L. Gray of Company E and Sergeant James Thomas Wolverton of Company G had been prisoners at various Confederate camps and were released in late April. Anxious to return to their families, they boarded the steamboat *Sultana* with other paroled Union soldiers going north. The steamboat was recklessly filled beyond capacity when its boiler exploded on the Mississippi River above Memphis on the night of April 27. It was the greatest maritime disaster in American history with some 1,700 passengers losing their lives. The three members of the Sixth Tennessee were among the survivors.[22]

Sergeant Wolverton recalled the events of that terrible night over fifty years later in a letter to the Memphis *Commercial-Appeal*. He wrote:

> I was stationed on harrican [*sic*] deck on the east side of the steamer near the center. Just behind me was a saloon and an ice chest [from which] the water was leaking…and had wet my blanket. So I decided I had rather remain up than attempt to sleep on a wet blanket…I had no other Place [*sic*] I could occupy…every available space I could see was occupied by the sleeping soldiers…While drearily slumbering there all at once I felt a terible [*sic*] shock followed by a deafning [*sic*] explosion, and before I could think my head struck water and I went

---

[20] TICW: 336. William M. Parker Civil War Questionnaire at TSLA.
[21] Colleen Morse Elliott and Louise Armstrong Moxley, eds. *Tennessee Civil War Veterans Questionnaires* (Easley, SC: Southern Historical Press, 1985): 1:101.
[22] Stephen Ambrose, "Remembering Sultana." *National Geographic*. (May 1, 2001). <news.nationalgeographic.com/news/2001/05/0501_river5.html>

down…strugling [*sic*] for breath. Finaly [*sic*] I [came] to the sur-
face exausted [*sic*] for breath. I began swiming [*sic*] the best I
could with my clothes and shoes on. I grabed [*sic*] at anything I
might get a holt [*sic*] on…At last I grasped some Peices [*sic*] of the
boat with my left arm, which was hardly sufficient to suport [*sic*]
me. A little later some pieces came up between my legs which
helped me to keep my head above water. I went whirling down
the river and soon landed in a drift with some others and went
whirling in a circle. We could see the burning wreck of the
steamer…Now I cannot think of that terable [*sic*] night…without
deep sorrow. Oh the terrible screams of the victims, which haunt
me when I hear it mentioned. It was like an old camp meeting before the war when the Preacher worked every soul up to
shouting.[23]

---

[23] James T. Wolverton Civil War Questionnaire at TSLA. Wolverton to Memphis *Commercial-Appeal*
editor, 29 January 1920. Ibid.

THIS SEEMS
TOO UNEQUAL

I N THE EARLY MONTHS OF 1865, Unionist leaders worked to ensure that only men of unquestionable loyalty would be in positions of civil and political authority in the state. They convened a de facto constitutional convention in Nashville on January 9 and with Andrew Johnson's approval took measures to bring Tennessee closer to a political reconciliation with the Union. An amendment was drafted to abolish slavery in the state and resolutions were passed that nullified its ordinance of secession and the acts of its Confederate government. The convention also nominated for governor William Gannaway Brownlow, a fiery Methodist preacher and East Tennessee newspaper publisher whose devotion to the Union bordered on fanatical, and assembled a slate of candidates for the General Assembly. Only voters who had participated in the 1864 Presidential election and sworn an oath of allegiance to the Union were eligible to vote in the referendum. Confederates soldiers and sympathizers were excluded from casting ballots.[1]

On February 22, state Unionists approved the referendum on the convention's initiatives including the abolition amendment to the state constitution, 25,293 to 48. Turnout was lower than anticipated but still met the ten percent requirement set by President Lincoln's amnesty proclama-

---

[1] Thomas B. Alexander, *Political Reconstruction in Tennessee* (Nashville, TN: Vanderbilt University Press, 1950): 30-31. E. Melton Coulter, *William G. Brownlow: Fighting Parson of the Southern Highlands* (Knoxville, TN: University of Tennessee Press, 1971): 260-261.

tion for citizens to take the oath of allegiance and seek admission back into the Union. A second election with over 23,000 votes cast validated Brownlow and the General Assembly candidates on March 4. Most eligible voters in West Tennessee were likely unaware the election was even being held. The instability of the region made it impossible to have ballot boxes in nineteen counties with the exception of Memphis and Shelby County. Because there was no opposition on the ballot, candidates for the General Assembly did not have to bother campaigning; their offices were virtually assured.[2]

Fielding Hurst was elected state senator representing the Twenty-First District, which was comprised of Hardeman, Hardin, and McNairy counties. He reached Nashville two days after the General Assembly convened on April 3. After taking the oath, his first act was to vote in favor of the ratification of the Thirteenth Amendment to the United States Constitution that prohibited slavery. He was appointed chairman of the Committee on Military Affairs and served as a member of the Elections and Judiciary committees.[3]

In his first message to the General Assembly on April 6, Governor Brownlow urged the new lawmakers to make right what their Confederate counterparts had done wrong in the state. "Secession is an abomination that I cannot too strongly condemn, and one that you cannot legislate against with too much severity," he believed.[4] During the nine-week session, legislators enacted a franchise law that set strict criteria for voter registration and barred ex-Confederates from the ballot box. The electorate was limited to men who were twenty-one years old since March 4, 1865, residents from other states who could prove their loyalty, and men of "unconditional Union sentiments from the outbreak of the rebellion until the present time." Former Confederate soldiers and sympathizers were restricted from voting for five years and Confederate officers and persons in positions of leadership for fifteen years.[5]

---

[2] Alexander, *Political Reconstruction in Tennessee*: 36, 38. The March 4 election was held in only 18 out of 30 counties in East Tennessee and 24 out of 35 counties in Middle Tennessee. Ibid 36.

[3] *Senate Journal of the First Session of the General Assembly of the State of Tennessee, 1865*. (Nashville: S.C. Mercer, 1865): 6, 15, 34

[4] *Report of the Joint Committee on Reconstruction at the First Session Thirty-Ninth Congress* (Washington D.C.: Government Printing Office, 1866): 13. <books.google.com>

[5] Alexander, *Political Reconstruction in Tennessee*: 74-75.

Hurst introduced seven bills, including ones to give the governor authority to raise troops to suppress guerrillas, change the boundary line between Hardin and Wayne counties to include one individual's home, and require that all civic officials in the state take an oath. One bill that became law permitted honorably discharged Union soldiers and loyal citizens to carry side arms to protect themselves and their property.[6] Needless to say, ex-Confederates throughout the state were very unhappy with the actions of what came to be known as the Brownlow Assembly, which acquiesced to much of the governor's vengeful agenda. "How does the Secesh enjoy things up your way[?]" sarcastically asked Hurst of his senate colleague Samuel R. Rodgers in Knoxville. "Taking it quiet down here [in McNairy County] but mad as hell."[7]

On the home front, the war was formally over but the hostilities between defeated Confederates and victorious Union soldiers continued in West Tennessee. A Memphis Unionist wrote President Andrew Johnson: "[T]here are *three* Rebels to *one* Union man [in West Tennessee], and it is as much as we can expect to be allowed to remain in the State. I tell you the fact that I am now on my good behavior to the returned Rebels, and have to shape my course not as I would, but as may be *expedient*."[8]

Good behavior did not always win favor with unreconstructed Rebels. Neighbors often harassed former Union soldiers and their families and attacked their homes in the middle of the night. "[M]any a man lies down at night uncertain whether or not his repose will be disturbed by the burning of his barn, or even of his dwelling," wrote a correspondent for the Nashville *Press*.[9] Such attacks were often met with retaliation. The same correspondent related how a search party riding through Lawrence, Perry, and Hardin counties in southwest Middle Tennessee "made an impression on three bushwhackers by firing a few slugs of lead through them, which it is hoped will keep them more quiet than the amnesty oath would."[10]

---

[6] Ibid: 54, 66, 68, 127, 137, 156-157, 161, 184. *Acts of the State of Tennessee Passed at the First Session of the Thirty-Fourth General Assembly for the Year 1865* (Nashville, TN: S.C. Mercer, 1865): 41-42.

[7] Hurst to Samuel R. Rodgers, 27 July 1865. O.P. Temple Papers.

[8] Current, *Lincoln's Loyalists*: 200

[9] "Troublous Times in West Tennessee." New York *Times*, 21 August 1865: 2. (Reprinted from the Nashville *Press*.)

[10] Ibid.

East Tennessee Unionists sought financial compensation through the courts against their rebel neighbors for acts of harassment, property theft, or violence during the war. Initially many plaintiffs won favorable verdicts and Governor Brownlow encouraged others across the state to file their own suits. Fielding Hurst enlisted the aid of fellow senator Samuel R. Rodgers to pursue a similar lawsuit on his behalf.[11] But the Federal courts eventually balked at the cases and took away a legal path for Unionists to pursue vindication for what had been done to them.[12] A wartime military commission had ruled that Brevet Brigadier General William J. Smith was entitled to reimbursement of $9,938.18 in property losses sustained to his Hardeman County plantation. Three subsequent orders decreed that the amount was to be levied against the citizens of Grand Junction, Tennessee, but President Andrew Johnson overruled the orders and suspended the collection.[13]

While Unionists were not allowed to sue former Rebels for damages or receive compensation for their losses, former Confederates were bringing their cases to Southern courts and many were receiving favorable verdicts.[14] Fielding Hurst was concerned for the plight of his fellow Unionists and wrote Governor Brownlow on July 26, 1865:

> The Secesh had their property taken by Federal authorities, and are now proving and collecting their claims at exorbitant prices, while the Union mens [sic] property was taken by rebel Soldiers and guirillas [sic] and Consequently have no available Source to look to for thier [sic] property or for pay. This Sir, Seems too unequal. I think there ought to be Some way or plan adopted by which union men can get pay for thier [sic] property...if not to deprive the Secesh of Collecting for theirs. The hardship is very

---

11 Hurst to Rodgers, 27 July 1865. O.P. Temple Papers.
12 Alexander, *Political Reconstruction in Tennessee*: 66-67.
13 PAJ 10: 344-345.
14 Current, *Lincoln's Loyalists*: 200. West Virginia was the only state that allowed Unionists to sue ex-Confederates for property losses. Ibid.

great and almost unlimited in this part of the Country and I think
is nearly all parts of the State.[15]

Brownlow forwarded Hurst's concerns to President Johnson, believing
"some relief" should be given to prevent "this great Injustice [*sic*]."[16] But the
new president, a champion of Tennessee Unionists as military governor,
now focused his attention on a peaceful and largely forgiving reconciliation
with the former Confederate states. On May 29, 1865, he issued an amnesty
proclamation that pardoned all except the wealthy and the high-ranking
Confederate civilian and military leaders upon taking an oath of allegiance to
the United States.[17] Yet his administration initiated no relief measures to aid
his former Unionist comrades. It was not until 1871 that Congress enacted
legislation for the Southern Claims Commission, an agency that spent ten
years reviewing applications from Southern loyalists and determining which
cases warranted compensation and to what degree.[18]

Governor Brownlow, on the other hand, carried out a much more
avenging policy against former Confederates in Tennessee while working to
return it to the Union. Congress determined that a seceded state must ratify
the proposed Fourteenth Amendment to the U.S. Constitution granting
African-Americans citizenship before being readmitted. The measure passed
the state senate but Brownlow's opponents in the house, determined to
prevent a quorum, would not come to the capitol building. The governor
had the missing representatives arrested and forcibly brought in for the
deciding vote. Thus Tennessee was readmitted to the Union on July 23,
1866 and spared the arduous Reconstruction policies inflicted upon the
other Southern states.[19]

But the harshness of Brownlow's dictatorial policies was too much for
some of his allies, who began speaking out against him and advocating the
restoration of voting rights to some ex-Confederates. The governor feared
he would lose his bid for re-election in 1867 and initiated his most controversial proposal to keep power: suffrage for African-American freedmen.
The General Assembly reluctantly passed the legislation, giving Tennessee

---

[15] Hurst to William G. Brownlow, 26 July 1865. Andrew Johnson Papers at TSLA.
[16] Ibid.
[17] Kenneth M. Stampp, *The Era of Reconstruction, 1865-1877*. New York: Vintage Books, 1965: 62-63.
[18] Ibid: 200, 208.
[19] Corlew, *Tennessee*: 333-334

the distinction of African-American suffrage almost three years before the ratification of the Fifteenth Amendment.[20]

------◄◄◆►►------

After his resignation as state senator[21], Fielding Hurst was appointed Circuit Judge for the Twelfth Judicial District in 1865. The district straddled the Tennessee River and included Decatur, Hardin, Henderson, Hickman, McNairy, and Wayne counties. He presided over the first postwar circuit court in McNairy County on July 10, 1865, which had not convened since March 13, 1862.[22]

Other members of the 6th Tennessee Cavalry won elected offices or received political appointments from Governor Brownlow as well. William J. Smith, who had been promoted to the rank of brevet brigadier general before the war ended, was a member of the January convention and was elected to the state legislature in 1865 and to the U.S. House of Representatives in 1868.[23] Major Stanford L. Warren became a member of the legislature even before he was honorably discharged. In 1867, President Johnson appointed him U.S. District Attorney for West Tennessee.[24] A deputy sheriff before the war, Captain Nathan McDonald Kemp became sheriff of Hardin County during Reconstruction.[25] Major Robert M. Thompson and Dr. Job Bell both served as county court clerks for McNairy County. Captain Samuel Lewis of Company A was appointed sheriff of McNairy

[20] Ibid: 334-335.
[21] Hurst resigned his senate seat between the end of the first session (June 12, 1865) and his first appearance on the bench in July 1865.
[22] *Report of the Joint Committee on Reconstruction, at the First Session of the Thirty-Fourth Congress.* McNairy County, Tennessee Circuit Court Minutes, Vol. A: 716.
[23] Robert M. McBride and Dan M. Robison, eds. Biographical Directory of the Tennessee General Assembly, Volume II: 1861-1901 (Nashville, TN: Tennessee State Library and Archives and Tennessee Historical Commission, 1979): 444. "Gen. W.J. Smith Falls Dead on the Street." Memphis Commercial-Appeal, November 30, 1913.
[24] Wright, *Reminiscences of McNairy County*: 13-14, 83.
[25] "Life of N.M.D. Kemp." Clifton (TN) *Mirror*, 16 June 1905. Kemp Family Chronicles website. 12 August 2007. <www.kempchronicles.com/doc.hmtl>

County and served for three years. Two years later James L.W. Boatman, another veteran of the regiment, was elected sheriff.[26]

———◆◄◉►◆———

The rule of Governor Brownlow and the Radical Republicans came to an end with the election of 1869 and the promise to give former Confederates the right to vote. The Franchise Law and other Brownlow legislation were dismantled and a new state constitution was ratified a year later.[27] Work began to rebuild the state's political, social, and economic structure shattered by eight years of war and Reconstruction.

Despite his financial and property losses, Fielding Hurst remained a wealthy man when the war ended. In addition to serving as a state senator and circuit judge, he also engaged in other activities during the period of Reconstruction. He owned a mill and practiced law in Purdy. He was among eighteen men who incorporated the Memphis City Railroad Company on June 7, 1865.[28] From 1867 to 1868, he served as a commissioner for the Freedman's Bureau in McNairy County. He donated land for a school in Purdy with 67 students that were taught by African-American teachers.[29] On February 16, 1870 he attended a reorganization meeting of the state Republican Party in Nashville intended to coordinate "resistance to the overwhelming tide of modern Rebel Democracy that is subverting all that is left of Republicanism in the Constitution and laws of the State." He was elected with G.W. Blackburn to represent the 6th District on the State Central Committee.[30]

---

[26] See Lewis' biographical sketch on page 120 for the circumstances of his death while serving as sheriff of McNairy County, Tennessee.

[27] Corlew, *Tennessee*, 342-351.

[28] *Acts of the State of Tennessee Passed at the First Session of the Thirty-Fourth General Assembly for the Year 1865* (Nashville, TN: S.C. Mercer, 1865): 88-90.

[29] Jonathan Kennon Thompson Smith, *Genealogical and Historical Gleanings from the Freedman's Bureau Records* (Jackson, TN: Self-published, 2003): 78. Hurst's title was Assistant Subassistant Commissioner. Records of the Field Offices for the State of Tennessee, Bureau of Refugees, Freedmen, and Abandoned Lands, 1865-1872.

[30] Fletcher, Andrew J. and J.O. Shackleford, The *Republican Party in Tennessee Reorganized*. (n.p., 1870). February 17, 2006 <books.google.com> 2, 4.

In his personal life, Hurst continued his wartime habit of seeking female companionship outside of his marriage. One such relationship with a young unmarried woman named Fancy Winters resulted in the birth of a daughter, Flora Temple Winters, on January 26, 1867. She was almost two years old before he legally recognized her and adopted her as his child.[31]

After stepping down as circuit court judge in 1869[32], Hurst was appointed collector of internal revenue for the Sixth District of Tennessee, a political appointment secured through President Ulysses S. Grant.[33] But he was removed in 1871 when subordinates fraudulently misappropriated funds for which he was held responsible.[34] This coupled with being held liable for unpaid security bonds crippled his personal finances. In 1876, he was forced to sell his two-story mansion in Purdy and move with his wife Melocky to their country home in the Mount Gilead community in northwest McNairy County. There he died on April 3, 1882 at about the age of 72 years old.[35]

Hurst was buried near his home at Mount Gilead Cemetery. Even in his grave, he found no peace from his enemies. It was reportedly desecrated on numerous occasions; men spit on it and had their horses tramp across it.[36] In the early 1900s, there was discussion that his remains might be reinterred at Shiloh National Cemetery but it was never realized.[37] For many years he had an unmarked grave; his niece eventually erected a headstone that identified him simply as "Judge F. Hurst" but with incorrect birth and death dates. Only a military marker at the foot of his grave, facing away from the cemetery's entrance, showed that he was Colonel Fielding Hurst of the 6th Tennessee (U.S.) Cavalry.[38]

---

[31] McNairy County, Tennessee Chancery Court Minutes: 85-86.
[32] Charles A. Miller, *The Official and Political Manual of the State of Tennessee* (Nashville, TN: Marshal and Bruce, 1890): 183.
[33] *Journal of the Executive Proceedings of the Senate of the United States of America.* Vol. 20: 15. Hurst's tenure lasted from December 1, 1869 to June 15, 1871.
[34] Ibid. Vol. 19: 623. Melocky Hurst Pension Application.
[35] Melocky Hurst Pension Application. Hurst's exact date of birth is not known.
[36] Blankenship, "Hurst": 86.
[37] "Col. Fielding Hurst." *McNairy County Independent*, 11 July 1902.
[38] Author's personal visit to Mount Gilead Cemetery, November 2006.

EPILOGUE

ORMER CONFEDERATE SOLDIER AND FORREST BIOGRAPHER John Allan Wyeth accurately described the condition of West Tennessee during the Civil War and the reasons for the atrocities committed by both sides there. "It is difficult for those who did not live through this unhappy period, and in this immediate section, to appreciate the bitterness of feeling which then prevailed," he explained. "Three years of civil war had passed, not without a deplorable effect upon the morals of the ranks and file of either army. War does not bring out the noblest traits in the majority of those who from choice or necessity follow its bloodstained paths. Too often the better qualities hide away, and those that are harsh and cruel prevail."[1]

The memories of Confederate soldiers and sympathizers as well as modern partisan historians have shaped how Colonel Fielding Hurst and the 6th Tennessee Cavalry are perceived today. They were branded as "home-made Yankees" and "a regiment of…predatory thieves, robbers, murderers and rapists" and quickly dismissed as cowards and traitors to the South.[2] The memories of Confederate soldier John Hallum provide a typical example of the way they have been portrayed:

> These renegade tories of southern blood preyed on the defense-
> less classes of west Tennessee, in the absence of nearly every able

---

[1] John Allan Wyeth, *That Devil Forrest: Life of General Nathan Bedford Forrest* (Baton Rogue: Louisiana State University Press, 1989): 338.
[2] Hallum, *Reminiscences*:: 10

bodied patriot, most of whom were in the Confederate armies fighting under the peerless leadership of General Forrest. The families of these absent veterans were singled out as objects of spoliation and plunder, and made victims of every species of crime. These outlaws to every noble sentiment were base born cowards, from their colonel down to the lowest travesty on manhood in his command...[3]

As this passage reflected, Confederate soldiers and civilians were regarded as noble and virtuous, unwilling to stoop to the methods of warfare practiced by "that demon called Hurst" and his "renegade tories." Yet history proves this to be untrue. Confederate soldiers and guerrilla bands were not above committing robberies, arson, and inhumane acts against Southern Unionists and civilians.

Fielding Hurst was a hated man not only for the choice he made, but also for the vengeful style of warfare in which he engaged. His tactics were not unlike what other Union forces used to combat Confederates, guerrillas, and even civilians. But he was a Southerner acting against his own people, which made it much more deplorable in their eyes. He became the embodiment of the "homemade Yankee."

Does Hurst deserve to be demonized as proponents of the Confederacy have done? It is true that he was not a leader to be revered. In his personal life, he was a man of questionable morals. He was an adulterer who brought women with him on military expeditions. Extortion under threat of the torch was a viable method of punishment and personal gain for him. By his words or actions, Confederate soldiers, guerrillas, and civilians were executed, often with barbaric and inhumane methods.

Yet Hurst's personal courage should also be acknowledged. He was willing to stand up for the Union when the majority around him sought to destroy it. He could have hid in the woods near his home or fled north as many others did to protect himself and his family from the threats and actions of his adversaries. Like some, he could have remained silent and stayed home; under his breath, he could have sworn allegiance to the Confederacy but secretly supported the Union. Instead he sought a military commission to raise a regiment of like-minded Southerners and help put down the rebellion. Whether it was pride or stubbornness, Hurst spoke out

---

[3] Ibid: 27.

against secession for which he was arrested, paraded in shackles and imprisoned like a criminal, tried in a Confederate court as a traitor, and sentenced to die.

Ironically, in a town that predominately favored the Confederacy during the war, it is the home of Fielding Hurst that still stands as the only period structure in what was once the thriving county seat called Purdy, Tennessee. But like the town itself, it has been abandoned in recent years and has deteriorated from neglect.

Hurst is inseparable from the 6th Tennessee Cavalry; one cannot discuss the regiment without mentioning the man who organized and led it. Thus the black mark often placed on him is also shared with the men under his command. Undoubtedly there were bad men in the 6th Tennessee who overstepped the bounds of "civilized" warfare and committed horrible crimes against soldiers away from the battlefield and civilians on the home front. Their military service was used as an excuse to settle private scores and exact revenge for past wrongs. The same can be said for their commanding officer as well.

Often it was the Unionist regiments that were directed to the front lines of the guerrilla warfare that was being waged in West Tennessee and north Mississippi. They were more familiar with the countryside, the terrain, and the people who lived there. But their participation also worsened the animosity that Confederates already held against them and presented them with opportunities to settle scores. Yet Hurst and his men did not corner the market on guerrilla-style tactics against soldiers and civilians in West Tennessee and North Mississippi. Confederate soldiers and citizens did not have hands as white as snow; theirs too were stained, but with the blood of men and women who remained loyal to the Union. Equally barbaric and ruthless tactics were used against them as well.

It would be wrong for modern readers to dismiss the regiment simply as a band of lawless thieves and murderers. They were not "independent partisan rangers" or an "irregular command" like their guerrilla adversaries, but were a commissioned cavalry regiment of the United States Army. They were brave men who had been persecuted by their families, friends, and neighbors for the stand they took. There were noble men in its ranks who fought because they felt secession or the institution of slavery was wrong. Most did so because they genuinely loved their country.

The American Civil War was a brutal and cruel conflict that affected not only the soldiers who fought on the battlefields, but also families and civilians on the home front. Lawless guerrillas terrorized the backwoods of West Tennessee and both Union and Confederate soldiers plundered food, livestock, and valuables from their homes and farms, leaving them destitute. The horrors of this period scarred a generation and the memories of that time were passed on to generations that followed. Even in the 21st Century, the name Fielding Hurst still stirs strong emotions for many of their descendants. For those who emphasize the glory of the Civil War, a study of the 6th Tennessee Cavalry and the warfare carried out in West Tennessee should prove to be a sobering reminder of the true nature of the conflict.

ROSTER

The following names of members of the 6th Tennessee Cavalry were taken from the *Report of the Adjutant General of the State of Tennessee of the Military Forces of the State from 1861 to 1866*.

Each soldier is a private unless otherwise noted. Every effort was made to compare and correct misspelled surnames to those contained in the Civil War Soldiers and Sailors System online database. Otherwise, names are spelled as they appeared in the *Report*.

Key
Bglr   Buglar
Bksm Blacksmith
CSgt   Commissary Sergeant
Cpl   Corporal
Lt   Lieutenant
QMS   Quarter Master Sgt
Sdlr   Saddler
Sgt   Sergeant
Tmtr   Teamster
Wgnr Wagoner

Field Staff

Colonels
Fielding Hurst
William J. Smith

Lieutenant-Colonels
William K.M. Breckenridge
William J. Smith
Orlando H. Shearer

Majors
William J. Smith
Daniel M. Emerson
Stanford L. Warren
Eldridge S. Tidwell
Thomas H. Boswell
Robert M. Thompson

Orlando H. Shearer
Mack J. Leaming

Surgeons
Thomas Williams
Jobe Bell (Assistant)
Pleasant A. Choshon (Assistant)
Joseph E. Marvin (Assistant)
Loomis O. Sumner (Assistant)

Chaplain
James J. Smith

Company A

Captains
Robert M. Thompson
Barney J. Riggs
Samuel Lewis

Drenney J. Archer (Cpl)
Newton O. Archer
Henry J. Baker
William H. Bashears
Asa Bell (1 Sgt)
William Bell
John Bivens
Joseph W. Bradshaw (Sgt)
Patrick Brannon
Henry H. Brickens
John Brown

Ninion T. Burchfield
Joseph Camdy
Robert C. Campbell
James H. Chamness
Robert Chandler
Peter M. Chesner (Sgt)
Thomas J. Cheshier (Cpl)
Henry S. Clines
Thomas H. Cobb (Cpl)
John Coleman (Cpl)
Rufus M. Coleman (Sgt)
Allen Cox
Edward Cox
Thomas Crangle (2 Lt)
William L. Crow (Sgt)
Charles Curtis
Henry Curtis
William Curtis
Columbus H. Deford (1 Lt)
Green D. Denny
Thomas Dickson
John B. Duke
Hezekiah Dunn
Hiram Dunn
John Dunn
William Dunn
Benjamin Esny (Bksm)
Stephen W. Fish
Henry V. Flowers
William Ford
John C. Fowler
Clindelin B. Furgison
Linsey Furgison
Joseph L. Gaice
Jasper L. Gann
Willis Gann
Thomas Gregg
Andrew Grisham
Issac Harris
Christopher C. Hester
Daniel Webster Hester (Sgt)
Enoch M. Hester
James W. Hester
Robert F. Hester
William E. Hester

Thomas Hodem
Somers B. Holeyfield
Sterling R. Horn
John Huddleston
Long B. Ivy
Issac P. Jandon
James B. Jernigan
John M. Lain (Sdlr)
Thomas M. Lain (1 Sgt)
Amsiah Laughlin
Calvin F. Laughlin
Lindy D. Laughlin
William Laughlin
William A. Laughlin
William R. Laughlin (Cpl)
William W. Laughlin
James R. Leonard (Sgt)
Peter S. Leonard
Robert H. Locke (Cpl)
George B. Maness
William R. Mathis
Issac T. Mathis
Lawson A. McIntire
William McIntire
Riley McVay
Joseph P. McVey
Rufus A. Monison
John Q.A. Monett
Dempsey W. Moore
Henry C. Moore
Jesse W. Moore (Cpl)
Marmaduke Murphy
George W. Oliver
William N. Ovardill
George M. Owens
William H. Owens
Samuel B. Ray
James T. Reams
Charles Reynoldsons
Jacob Richardson
John H. Riley
Joseph M. Rise
George W.M. Robertson
Thomas L. Robertson
Mark M. Rose (Bglr)

William Jasper Newton Rose
Ayer R. Russom
George W. Russom
John J.R. Russom
William J. Russom
Issac H. Sellers
Robert S. Sewell
James T. Singleton (Cpl)
George T. Smith
Issac A. Smith
James J. Smith (1 Lt)
John H. Smith
John Spencer
Clayton Stewart (Bglr)
James S. Stewart
William Stone
Chris C. Swain
Joseph J. Swain
William H. Swain (2 Lt)
William Thomas
George Vaughn
John Vaughn
Nathan Vaughn
John Wards
James H. Wasdin
Thomas F. Waters
James R. Westbrooks
Jesse Wilson
John R. Wilson
Robert A. Wilson
William A. Wilson
William P. Wilson (Cpl)
James Wolverton
Richard T. Wolverton (Sgt)
James W. Wright
John C. Wright
Franklin A. Young

Company B

Captains
Harry Hodges
Elijah J. Hodges
James Ballard
Charles L. Barham (Cpl)

Drew (or Driver) F. Bassham
Eli F. Bassham
James W. Bassham
Richard A. Bassham
Pleasant M. Beaty
Robert M. Beaty
David M. Beck
Grear Blakely (Sgt)
James P. Blakely (1 Sgt)
James L.W. Boatman
John H. Boo
John William Bradley (Sgt)
James Brake
George N. Bullman
Andrew J. Burkhead
Elazer B. Burkhead
William S. Chamness
William A. Clark
James M. Clayton
Elijah N. Clemmons
Thomas H. Cobb
John Connor
Charles B. Covey (Sgt)
Samuel J. Cox
William M. Crow (Sgt)
Sullivan Cyes
George M. Denison
John L. Dickey
John M. Dunn (Cpl)
Richard W. Eskridge (2 Lt)
Frederick J. Floyd
John Taylor Gage
Turner C. Goodram
Alexander Grear
Haywood Hair
Jorden C. Halstead (Cpl)
Samuel D. Hanna (1 Lt)
Henry Harris
Chapel Heath
James S. Henderson
John R. Henderson
John B. Hicks
Elias J. Highsmith
John W. Highsmith
John Huddleston (2 Lt)

Joel H. James
Francis Jeter
William C. Johnson (Cpl)
George W. Kernodle
William Kerr
William W. Kirby (2 Lt)
Harvig Knotts (Cpl)
John T. Knotts
David C. Lee
William S. Lee
John M. Lowrance (Sgt)
Thomas Macon
George D. Maness (Cpl)
Constant T. Massey
David H. Massey
James C.J. Maxwell (Sgt)
John W. McClure (Sgt)
William C. McClure
Issac T. McIntyre
Thomas V. Moss
Charles Murine
Hugh S. Patterson
Britton A. Phillips
William R. Phillips
William Piggett (Sgt)
Jacob M. Pike
Abraham Plunk
George M. Plunk
Joseph A. Plunk
Jacob S. Plunk
Miles Plunk
Peter Plunk
John F. Putman (Sgt)
Francis M. Rankin
John Ray (Bglr)
Needham B. Rayford
John T. Riggs (Sdlr)
Nelson C. Riggs
John Rodgers
William W. Russell
Jesse E. Sanders
Joel D. Sanders
John F. Sharp
John W. Sheffield (Cpl)
Abraham Sipes

John Sipes (Cpl)
John L. Smith
Madison Smith
William F. Smith
John F. Stewart
Amzier C. Sweat
James L. Sweat
Newton J. Sweat (Cpl)
James R. Thacker (Cpl)
Joseph G. Thomas
Stephen J. Thomas
William Tidwell
Francis M. Tucker (1 Lt)
George W. Tucker (Bksm)
John Viess
Samuel Viess
William Viess
Benjamin T. Walker
Samuel L. Walker
William C. Walker
Thomas H. Ward
Thomas J. Warsham
William T. White
Fidler S. Whitman
Sebern L. Whitman
Peter H. Whitt
Samuel R. Whitt
Joseph E. Wilkerson (Tmtr)
Andrew J. Williams
Archibal B. Womble (Cpl)
William Wren
John S. Yolverton
Rufus N. Young

Company C

Captain
Nathan McDonald Kemp

George Adams (Sgt)
William C. Adams
Benjamin F. Alexander (Sgt)
Robert L.P. Alexander
John Allen
George W. Anderson (Cpl)

William R. Anderson
Thomas A. Ansley
William Austin
Gary Bartley
Rufus N. Bass
William M. Bethune
Green Brown
George W. Bryant (Sgt)
William Burl
Samuel P. Campbell (Cpl)
Elias J. Carter (Sgt)
John Chalk
James L. Cherry
Thomas G. Clary
John Coley
Thomas Crangle (1 Lt)
Walter C. Crow
Walter C. Crownover
Thomas Davis
James M. Dickson
Kendred M. Dodds
Thomas J. Farris
Jacob M. Ford
James L. Glenn
Yancey W. Gray
John Furgerson (Cpl)
William E. Haddon (Sgt)
Wiley B. Haile
James C. Hailey
James H. Ham
Monroe Ham
Harrison L. Harbert (1 Sgt)
Henry C. Harbert
Terrill P. Harbert (Sgt)
Blackman J. Hardin
Samuel G. Harvell
Newton C. Hawkins
William H.F. Hennings
Christopher W. Hoffer
Thomas R. Holley
William H. Hughes
William M. Hutcherson
William H. Hyatt
George Johnson
Henry M. Johnson

Benjamin S. Jones
David W. Jones
George W. Jones (Sgt)
Jackson A.J. Jones
John W. Jones (Sgt)
Josiah Jones
Richard C. Jones
Samuel H. Jones
Edward Elemuel Kemp (Sgt)
Joseph Warren Kemp (Sgt)
David Kennedy
Issac Kennedy
Samuel M. Kerr
James C. Landreth
James C. Lee
John R. Lewis
Jesse K. Little
David C. Lowery
William M. Mallory
Benjamin Martin
Thomas G. McBride (Cpl)
James C. McCauley
William S. McClintock
James P. McFerrin
James R. Meddow
Jonas Meddow
George Medlin
Amziah T. Meek
David J. Montgomery (Sgt)
John Mooney
Marcus Morney
Elijah Morris
George Moss
Marcus W. Moss
Medrith (or Meredith)
P.G. Nickins
Allen T. Nolen (Cpl)
Barry Nolen
Lewis Outlaw
William M. Outlaw
William J. Parker
Thomas Phillips
Nicholas M. Phillips (Cpl)
William W. Phillips
Matthew Pickens

John W. Plunk
Bradley Polk
Wiley J. Priddy
James R. Purkins
James L. Randolph
Malicah W. Randolph
Barney J. Reden (Cpl)
Abraham G. Ricketts
George W. Robertson
Joseph M. Robertson (Sgt)
Lewis W. Robins
William R. Robins
Thomas A. Ross (Cpl)
John Rowsey
James M. Sanders (2 Lt)
Wiley T. Sanders
Joseph Sanderson (Sgt)
William R. Sanderson
William J. Scroggins
John R. Sherley
Lacenas M. Shutts
John N. Singleton
Sterlin Singleton
Calwell P. Smith
William Smith (1 Lt)
George W. Sturdivant
Harsn N. Sturdivant
Thomas J. Sturdivant
William J. Sturdivant
John H. Taylor (Sgt)
Eldridge S. Tidwell (Sgt)
John F. Tidwell
John W. Tidwell
Richard F. Tucker
Franklin Turner
Duncan B. Vandike
John L. Vinson
James C. Washburn
John E. Watson
Josiah A. Watson (Cpl)
Jasper Wicker
Solomon G. Williams (Cpl)
William Willis
James Wilson
Benjamin F. Winchester

Company D

Captains
James L.W. Boatman
Levi Hurst

James Adams
William Anglin
Stephen J. Barber
Thomas J. Barber
William F. Barber
Frederic A. Barns
Benjamin F. Barton
George H. Basinger
Napoleon B. Bennich
Preston B. Bourland
Azariah L. Boyd
James T. Boyd
Franklin Brack
Lewis C. Brandon (Sgt)
Charles M. Brooks
Enoch Caruth (Sgt)
Benjamin F. Carter (Cpl)
Issac Clark
Jesse M. Clark
Jackson Clinton
William P. Cook
Matthew Croniga
James W. Crouch
Carroll Crumby
Hugh Crumby
John W. Curry (Sgt)
William J. Dancer
Thomas J. Dick
Charles M. Dodd
Jason Dodd
John M. Dodd (Cpl)
Samuel D. Dodd
William R. Dodd
Hezekiah Dyson
Annanias O. Eliff
William Findly
Thomas J. Fisher
George W. Flake
Sampson F. Flake (Cpl)

Benjamin Fortner
Laney Fowler
Thomas J. Fox (Sgt)
John Gann
William Gattis
Andrew H. Gibbons
Ebenezer F. Gibbons
John P. Gibbons (1 Lt)
Cornelius T. Gore
Cornelius Graham
John D. Graham
Randolph Graham
Charles Griffin
Joel J. Griffin
John J. Hall
William F. Hance
William Harden
Energy P. Hardwitch
James L. Hardwitch (2 Lt)
William C. Henderson
Abraham Hollaway
James Hollaway
William Hollaway
Calvin A. Holley
William S. Holly
David Horn
James F. Horn (1 Cpl)
James R. Horn
Stephen Horn
William J. Horn (Sgt)
Willis R. Horn (Bksm)
Jacob Hosier
George W. Howell
George W. Hubanks
Elihu De Grasse Hurst
Doctor Reader Hurst
Jonathan Blake Hurst
William De Lafayette Hurst (Sgt)
Carroll James
James H. Jenkins
Stephen Jones
John A. Lackey (1 Lt)
Joseph D. Little
Lorenza D. Lovell
James R. Manuel

John R. Martin
Moses M. Martin (Sgt)
Samuel G. Martin
William J. Matthews
John T. McCaleb (Sgt)
Hezekiah McNatt
Thomas R. McNatt
William McNatt
David C. Mitchell
John P. Mitchell
Hiram J. Moore
Samuel Moore
John A. Morgan
John B. Morgan
Abraham Myers (Cpl)
Thad C. Newcomb
James R. Norcutt (1 Lt)
Zachariah Norcott (1 Lt)
Thomas M. Palmer
Levi Pierce
Madison Powell
John W. Ramer
Thomas J. Randolph
Samuel W. Riggs
Lewis J. Schrismer
William B. Simpson
William H. Stiles
Martin V. Stocton
Harvey A. Taylor
Josiah Thomason
Relius B. Trim
John M. Tuly (1 Sgt)
Albert C. Wallace
Benjamin F. Wallace (Cpl)
Littleton Wallace
Streeton C. Wallace
Thomas S. Wallace
James M. Ward (Bglr)
Alfred F. Whitehurst
Oliver S. Whitehurst (Cpl)
George W. Wolf
Henry A. Wolf
Peter W. Wolf
James M. Wylie

Company E

Captains
Francis Smith
John D. Poston

Doctor Z. Alexander
Francis A. Alexander
Christopher R. Allen (Cpl)
Columbus R. Allen (Cpl)
Ryal D. Allen
Charles Andrewson
Richard A. Atkinson
William Atkinson
Anderson Bailey
James D. Barchum
James Baty
George Box
Green L. Britt
Edward H. Brown (Cpl)
Jackson Brown
Christopher C. Burchum
John A. Burchum
David M. Burton
Thomas S. Burton
William S. Carnell
John J. Cash (Sgt)
Berim'n R. Chambers (Cpl)
Ezra Cheany (Sgt)
James C. Childress
James M. Christenberry
John A. Clark
William Clery (2 Lt)
John H. Cofer
Frank Collins
John M. Condrn
Jasper Cosart
George W. Craig
William E. Curtis
Martin V. Day
Milas M. Deason (Bglr)
Joseph L. Deweese
George H. Dunn
David B. Edsen
George L. Ellis (Sgt)

Henry Ethridge
Daniel Floyd
William R. Fourshee
Nathan G. Foulkes
John H. Gailes (Cpl)
James W. Gibson
Hubbard P. Greathouse
John N. Green
Joseph M. Green
Pilcher H. Gregory
Thomas M. Hardison
Oren M. Harlen
Benjamin F. Hawkins
Jasper Henderson
Hugh A. Hill (Cpl)
Noah H. Hill
Daniel Hooper
Samuel Hubbs
Issac Jackson
Joseph James (Sgt)
David M. Johnson
William E. Johnson (1Sgt)
William R. Johnson
Anderson Jones
James Jones
Frederick N. Kelso
Benjamin W. King
George W. Kirk
Sidney E. Kirk
Andrew J. Knight
Isiah Lavely
Issac J. Leadbetter
Alexander Lewis
Charles Lewis
Frederick Lewis
James A. Lewis
Thomas Lofties
Jason Lonan
Valentine Matheny
Ranel P. McGnorter
Thomas J. McMurry
James P. Meadows
Andrew J. Medlin
Charles W. Meeker
Alfred Middleton

Benjamin F. Miller (Bksm)
Thomas Miller
John A. Mills (C Sgt)
Andrew J. Moore
John T. Neel
James K.P. Neely
James W. Neely
Robert W. Nelson
James Nolan
Joseph M. Nuckols
Robert M. Pankey
Richard A. Parks
James M. Pate
Francis M. Peck
David Peterson
James B. Phipps
John W. Pickens
James W. Pulley (Sgt)
James L. Randolph
Daniel H. Rankin
John F. Ray
Alexander Reimers (Sdlr)
Berry J. Rodgers
Thomas Ruffin
Daniel Ryan
Stephen W. Satterfield (QSM)
Edward Scarbrough
John W. Shelton
James Sheveton
John C. Simmons
William Simmons
James D. Sloan
David Sneed
David Spiva
Daniel Stamps
John T. Stamps
John W. Stansberry
William J. Stephens (Cpl)
James E. Stewart
Levi J. Stout
Carroll Sweeny
Doctor T. Talley
Archie F. Taylor
David A. Taylor
Emerson S. Taylor

James A. Taylor
Henry Thomas
James B. Thompson
Simpson H. Viah (Bglr)
Jeremiah M. Walker
John B. Walker
Charles J. Wallace (Cpl)
James W. Walls
John A. Waters
James H. Webb
William Weeks
Henry P. Wilkins
Robert L. Williams
William F. Williams
William Woodard (Cpl)
Miles M. Woodside

Company F

Captain
David J. Dickerson

James N. Alexander
Grand H. Alexander
Robert M. Alexander
Benjamin F. Arnold
James Arnold
John Austin
William H. Battles
David B. Beckham
Finley S. Beckham (Sgt)
Robert P.O. Boswell (1 Lt)
Wesley Boyd
John Branom (Cpl)
William Branom
Thomas J. Breckenridge
James J. Bryant
John Bryant
Francis M. Clay
John A. Clay
James M. Clayton
Stephen H. Clayton (Sgt)
Jackson L. Clifton
Nathan Clifton
Andrew Cole

Franklin Cole
William Cole
Robert Cooper (Cpl)
William H. Cooper
William Crofford
Thomas A. Cummings
Daniel E. Daily
Daniel D. Davis
George W. Davis, Sr.
George W. Davis Jr.
William B. Davis
William H. Davis
Barkly Dearow
George W. Duncan
John Dixon
John Edwards
William Ferrell
John Franks
Peter Frayoner
Samuel Gellorthan
Henry C. Gibbs
John R. Gibbs
Barnabas Gifford
Levi Gifford
Edward W. Gobble
Berry Green (Cpl)
Robert N. Grimes (Cpl)
Edward L. Hardin (1 Lt)
Benjamin F. Hasty
Samuel M. Haynes (Sgt)
George T. Helton (Sgt)
Henry A. Helton
James W. Helton (1 Sgt)
Isaac B. Hobbs
James L. Hobbs
Henry Horton
James Horton (Tmsr)
John E. Horton
Issac James (Cpl)
Louis C. Johnson
Daniel D. Judd
Andrew W. King
David Kooch
Franklin V. Laker
George W. Lawson

John M. Lawson
Mordecai S. Lawson
John C. Linn
Henry Long
Erwin Loyed
James Mathis
Daniel K. McGee
William H. McGee
Andrew J. McWilliams (Sgt)
James A. McWilliams
John Melson
William Morris
Alvin G. Moss
Francis Newborn (Cpl)
William N. Newsom
Hauten's C. Newton
George W. Morris (Cpl)
George Peck
John Price
John A. Prince (Sgt)
William Prince
Josiah J. Pritchett
Andrew J. Quails
Owen Quails (Cpl)
James Ray
Dennis C. Roberts
John H. Robins
Calvin Rose
David G. Rose
John Rose
William C. Rose
George Sanders (Cpl)
Louis Scaggs
John W. Scott
Richard D. Scott (Cpl)
William A. Shands (Tmsr)
John Shoebert
James E. Smith
John A. Smith
Joseph J. Smith
Emsley Tacker
Levi Thompson (Sgt)
Michael L. Thrasher
Bennett D. Todd
John Turnbow (Bglr)

William Waldrop (Cpl)
George W. Walker (Sgt)
Benjamin G. White
Dempsey White (Cpl)
Pleasant C. Whitworth (Sgt)
John Willbanks
Richard Willbanks
John Wooley
John W. Youngblood (2 Lt)

COMPANY G

Captains
William Chandler
William C. Webb

John W. Adair
James Adams
Thomas P. Alexander
Barkley M.D. Allen (Cpl)
William O. Avrett (Sgt)
James L. Bagsby
Benjamin Baker (Cpl)
Robert Banks
William F. Barber
Stephen J. Barber
Thomas J. Barber
Alexander Barnes
Frederick A. Barnes (Sgt)
Robert J. Barnes
William Beard (Blkm)
William Bird
Franklin Brack
James M. Bradford
Robert W. Brashear (Cpl)
William Brown
Asa W. Bryant
James L.W. Boatman (1 Lt)
William F. Boatright (2 Lt)
Pleasant Bureham
Archa Burleyson
John Burleyson
Jonathan Burleyson
Enoch Caroth
Balis S. Carr

Elisha Chandler
Jesse J. Demons
William P. Cook
Rufus King Cooper
Matthew Cronaga
John Davis
Lewis Davis
Thomas J. Dick
Elias Dodson
James M. Dodson (Sgt)
William Eason
Benjamin F. Edmonds
Galloway H. Edmonds
Jerome Edmonds
William P. Essary (Sdlr)
George W. Fowler
John D. Fowler
Laney Fowler
Ed M.V. Furgison
James H. Furgison (Cpl)
Martin V.B. Gainnss
William J. Gander
Andrew H. Gibbins
John R. Gibbs
John A. Gill
Jones K, Gill (Sgt)
Samuel K. Gill (Bksm)
Cornelius Graham (Sgt)
Randolph Graham
William A. Grant
James M. Graves
John P. Graves
William C. Graves
Morgan L. Gray (Cpl)
Jones J. Griggs
Hugh K. Guthrie
John K. Guthrie
Robert A. Guthrie
Thomas M. Guthrie
James P. Haggard
John H. Hamilton
William F. Hance
Samuel D. Hanna (1 Sgt)
William Harrington
Joseph W. Harris

William M. Haynes
William C. Henderson
David Herron
William Holland
Riley Homes
Willis R. Horn
James H. Jenkins
Robert Jordan
Jackson J. King
William H. Kilpatrick
John Kyle (Bglr)
John H. Lard
Robert W. Ledbetter
Lazy D. Lemons
Burrel Liles
Wesley W. Liles (Cpl)
John E. Littell
George W. Little
Issac Little
Issac L. Longwith
Alex H. Lowrance
Hardin L. Lyons
Joseph Martin
Ezra R. Marvin
William J. McAnolly
James F. McCann
Wade B. McCassland
Hezekiah K. McNatt
Thomas R. McNatt
Erving C. Medlin
Isham M. Miller
Sineth H. Moore
George Morgan
Anderson Mozier
Jacob Mozier
Buckner K. Murphy
Calvin B. Murphy
Clement J. Murphy
Abraham Myers
Charner H. Neely
Joseph Newsom
William A. Newsom
Ambrose P. Nipper
Oliver M. Norman
James I. Ore

Calvin Ozment
John D. Ozment
William H. Parish
Wesley W. Parker
David W. Patterson
Thomas E. Pegram
John Wesley Plunk (Cpl)
Peter Plunk
Madison Powell
John W. Ramer
James M. Ray
John R. Ray (2 Lt)
John C. Reynolds
Thomas E. Reynolds
Joseph W. Riggs
Nelson C. Riggs (Sdlr)
James M. Riley
Houston Roberts (Sgt)
Philip Roberts
Wyley M. Roberts
James W. Rollins
James W. Rose
Edwin R. Rushing (1 Sgt)
Elijah B. Rushing
Joel P. Rushing
Richard Rushing
George R. Sewel
Olynthees G. Shelton
Issac J. Shull(2 Lt)
William B. Simpson
John A. Sipes
William J. Smith
William Smallwood
William C. Stanfield
William H. Stiles
Alfred Swain
William J. Swain
Laney M. Sweat (Cpl)
Willis I. Sweat (Sgt)
Leroy J. Tacker
James K.P. Taylor
Jerry M. Terry
James Thomas
Arthur Tolly
Andrew J. Treas

David E. Tucker
Rufus D. Wade
Elias G. Walker
James Ward
George T. Ware (Sgt)
Elijah F. Warren
Samuel H. Weabroocks
Zachariah West
Henry Williams
Henry C. Williams
William F. Williams
Hezekiah Wilson
George W. Wolf
Henry A. Wolf
Peter W. Wolf
James T. Wolverton
James R. Wright
Allen Yelvington
James I. Young
Rufus N. Young

COMPANY H

Captains
Joseph G. Berry
Risden D. Deford

Benjamin L. Allen (Cpl)
Edward F. Ansley
Wesley M. Ansley (Sgt)
Henry A. Archer
William P. Austin
Elijah Battle
William H. Battles
James E. Berry
James W. Boling (Bksm)
William M. Bonds
Thomas P. Boyd
William W. Boyd
Ira J. Brown
James H. Carson
Joshua Carter (Sgt)
Asy G. Chism
James M. Clayton
William Crawford

Thomas A. Cummings
Thomas D. Davidson
George W. Davis (Cpl)
James H. Davis
James J. Davis (1 Sgt)
William B. Davis
William H. Davis
Columbus H. Deford
Alexander Earnest
Benjamin F. Farmer
John W. Gallion
William Gallion
Thomas J. Garner
Bartly Gary (Cpl)
Henry H. Gibbs
Jonathan D. Gillis (Sgt)
Zachariah T. Goldsmith
Squire Haggard
Gabriel D. Halaway
Calvin Hana (1 Lt)
John H. Hanserd
George R. Harrison
William R. Hendricks
John L. Holden
Carroll H. Hulin
William G. Hugs
James A. James (Cpl)
Jesse James
John H. James (2 Sgt)
Robert H. Jurdin
Jonathan J. Keeton
James H. Kiddy
Jacob P. Lackey
William M. May
William J. McAusley (S Ser)
Wade B. McCasland
James P. McConel (Cpl)
William H. McGee (Cpl)
William J. McKennon
James H. McKey (Sgt)
Joseph Montgomery
William A. Newsom (2 Lt)
John A. Nichols (Cpl)
William C. Nichols
Ambrose P. Nipper

Marion J. Osbern
Samuel H. Parker
William R. Parsons (Sgt)
Jacob J. Pevyhouse
Jacob L. Phillips
Nicholas Pitts (2 Lt)
Francis M. Pool
George W. Pool
John R. Pool
Joseph Pritchett
Wiliam L. Packard
Anderson Ray
Moses Ray
Able A. Reed (5 Sgt)
Issac W. Reed
Calvin Rose
Jeremiah Rawlings
John W. Robinson
Franklin M. Robison
Robert L. Saxan
Henry Sexan
James C. Shull
Paul A. Sims
William Skaggs
James A. Smith (Cpl)
James C. Smith
Jasper W. Smith
Richard Smith
William M. Smith
William H. Stennett
James L. Stricklin
Peter Stricklin
William H. Stricklin
Joseph J. Suna (Buglr)
David R. Tapkel
Pugh H. Thrasher
James L. Tidwell
John Tidwell
William C. Tidwell
Michael J. Thrasher (Cpl)
Lafayette Townsley
William W. Walker
George W. Wallace
Andrew Weaver
Jacob J. Weaver

James Webb
William Webb
James H. Wesson
Randolph Wesson
Zachariah West (Wgnr)
James P. Wilks (Cpl)

COMPANY I

Captains
Orlando H. Shearer
Stanford L. Warren

James Adams
Guss A.H. Allmon (Sgt)
John F. Allmon (Sgt)
William Anglin
John H. Baker
Miles R. Baker
Stephen J. Barber
Thomas J. Barber
William F. Barber
Frederic A. Barns
Benjamin F. Barton
George H. Basinger
John R. Baughman
Hurbert Bell
Seldon Bell
Napoleon B. Bennich
Edward Bigger
Madison Billingsby
Azariah L. Boyd
James T. Boyd
Franklin Brack
John A. Brann (Sgt)
Coleman Brann
Henry B. Brann
Telmon Brann
Charles M. Brooks
Coloin Brundridge
James L. Bullington
John R. Byars
John S. Callison
William R. Callison (Sgt)
Edward Campble (Bglr)

William J. Campbell (1 Lt)
George W. Cantrell
William Cantrell
Benjamin F. Carter (Cpl)
Marshall V. Carter
Parham Carter
Pinkney Carter
Enoch Caruth (Sgt)
Benjamin F. Clark
Issac Clark
Jesse M. Clark
Jonathan L. Cooly (Cpl)
William P. Cook
Matthew Croniga
James W. Crouch
Carroll Crumby
Hugh Crumb
William J. Dancer
Andrew D. Denning (Cpl)
Thomas J. Dick
Charles M. Dodd
Jasin Dodd
John M. Dodd (Cpl)
Samuel D. Dodd
William R. Dodd
Hezekiah Dryson
John H. Eaves
John A. Edwards (Sgt)
Annanias O. Elliff
William Findly
George W. Fiske
James M. Flake
Sampson F. Flake (Cpl)
Leander J. Foster
James M. Foster
Laney Fowler
Bernjamin Fortner
Philip N. Frazier
John Gann
Randolph C. Gantee
Calvin Gatewood
Henry Gatewood
Lawson Gatewood
Pinkney Gatewood
William Gattis

Andrew H. Gibbons
Ebenezer F. Gibbons
Daniel B. Gliason
George W. Glisson
William H. Glisson
Henry C. Golden
Cornelius T. Gore
Solomon W. Gore
Thomas J. Goskins
Elijah L. Graham (Sgt)
Charles Griffin
Joel J. Griffith (Cpl)
Cornelius Graham
John D. Graham
Randolph Graham
William F. Hance
William Harden
James R. Harris
Robert R. Hart
William C. Henderson
Energy P. Hardwitch
James L. Hardwitch (2 Lt)
Abraham Hollaway
James Hollaway
William Hollaway
Calvin A. Holly
William S. Holly
David Horn
James R. Horn
Stephen Horn
James F. Horn (1 Cor)
Willis R. Horn (Bksm)
Jacob Hosier
James M. Humphrey
Doctor Reader Hurst
Elihu R. Hurst
John Hurst
Levi Hurst
Carroll James
David N. Johnson
James H. Jenkins
Stephen Jones
Crocket M. Kimbrel
Francis M. Kimbrel
Henry H. Kimbrel

William R. Kimbrel
John W. King
John A. Lakey (Sgt)
Henry M. Laurence
Columbus W. Lee
Pinkney W.H. Lee
Joseph D. Little
Larry F. Long
Curta D. Lovelace
Lorenza D. Lovell
Tobias Lawry
James R. Manuel
John R. Martin
Moses Martin
Samuel G. Martin
Francis M. Mathena
James Mathena
William J. Matthews
Stith Maynord
William H. Maxey
Hezekiah McNatt
Thomas R. McNatt
William McNatt
David C. Mitchell
John P. Mitchell
Hiram J. Moore
Samuel Moore
James Morgan
John A. Morgan
John B. Morgan
John G. Morgan
Abraham Myers (Cpl)
Madison F. Newberry
Thad C. Newcomb
Robert Newton
James R. Norcott (1 Lt)
Zachariah Norcott (1 Lt)
Benjamin Oliver
William A. Osborn (Cpl)
James M. Palmer
Thomas M. Palmer
Vaden C. Parrish
Levi Pierce
Daniel W. Pounds
John H. Pounds

Madison Powell
Pleasant L. Powers
James W. Price
Willis J. Price
John W. Ramer
Thomas J. Randolph
James F. Richardson
Samuel Richardson
John B. Roberts
Reuben D. Roberts
William A. Roberts
Preston B. Rourland
James W.H. Ryold
Lewis J. Schrimsher
William F. Sigamore
William B. Simpson
Coleman D. Smith
John W. Smith
William J. Staker
James M. Stell
Samuel S. Stell
William H. Stiles
Martin V. Stocton
Boliver M. Stone
Issac C. Stone
John H. Tanner
Harvey A. Taylor
Josiah Thomason
Eli Todd
Lewis Todd
William N. Todd
Relius A. Trim
John S. Turner
Albert C. Wallace
Banjamin F. Wallace (Cpl)
Littleton Wallace
Streeter S. Wallace
Thomas S. Wallace
William M. Wallace
James M. Ward (Bglr)
Alfred F. Whitehurst
Benjamin D. Whitehurst
Enoch H. Whitehurst
Oliver S. Whitehurst (Cpl)
Caleb J. Wilson

George W. Wolf
Henry A. Wolf
Miles Wood (2 Lt)
George W. Wright
James M. Wylie
John F. Zearnger

COMPANY K

Captains
Thomas H. Boswell
Albert Cook

Aaron G. Allmond
Dempsey B. Arnold
Hosea G. Arnold
Francis A.M. Atkinson
James M. Atkinson
Thomas A. Atkinson (Sgt)
Daniel R. Baldridge
James T. Barham (Cpl)
John W. Barham (1 Lt)
Charles H. Batt
Reuben H. Beazley (Sgt)
Thomas Y. Beard
John F.M. Blacknall
Charles R. Bostick
William A. Bostick (Bglr)
Robert F.O. Boswell (1 Sgt)
Emerson E. Bowers (Cpl)
James E. Bowers (1 Sgt)
John F.M. Bowers (Sgt)
Edmond T. Bradberry
James B. Bradberry
John H. Bradberry (Cpl)
John C. Brandon
James T. Brogdon
William Brogdon
Robert H. Bullington
Jesse F. Butcher
William D. Butts
David F. Campbell
Horatio L Cannon
Henry W. Caraway
Christopher B. Clark

John T. Climer
Henry C. Craig
John Crutchfield
Samuel M. Damron
James W. Davis
James M. Dickerson
Richard W. Dorch
John Dyer
William R. Eves
Malloy E. Foster
Rufus H. Fowler
John M. Glisson
David S. Hedgepeth
Andrew J. Higgs
George W. Higgs
Patrick G. High
John S. Hornsby
William Huffman
Thomas F. Hutchins
Zachariah Hutchins
Constant W. Hynds (QMS)
David R. Hynds (Cpl)
George W. Irby
James J. Levister (Sgt)
William F. Levister
James P. Mathis
Jesse O. Mathis
James E. McNair (1 Lt)
Thomas B. Miller
William N. Mitchell
John W. Moore
William E. Moore
George W. Murphy (Cpl)
James M. Murphy (Cpl)
George W. Norman
James M. Palmer
Avery Parham
John H. Parker (Sgt)
Zachariah Parker
Charles A. Parrott
Lewis G. Parrott
James P. Peel
Marquis L. Peery
John W. Petree
Clem Pierce

John W. Powers
Elijah R. Reavis (C Sgt)
Leonidas W. Reavis (Cpl)
William M. Richards
George W. Somers
Benjamin M. Smith
St. Clair W. Smith
William J. Stafford
Joseph M. Taylor
Robert H. Taylor (Sgt)
William H. Taylor
William J. Taylor
William L. Tuck
Harrison W. Vowel (Bksm)
William J. Vowel
Thomas C. Warren
Francis E. Welch
George T. Welch
Alexander D. Weldon
William H. Weldon
Amasa J.T. Wilson
Rolla F. Wilson
John R. Winston
John V. Woodruff
Marcellus Woodruff

COMPANY L

Captains
John H. Edwards
John W. Moore

Andrew M. Alexander
Ucbia (or Uclid) D. Allen
John A. Allman
Elijah Arnold
Elisha Arnold
Ezikel Arnold
Henry P. Barbee
Robert Beard
Churchill E. Bondurant
William G. Bowers
James A. Briganee
John A. Briganee
William C. Brooks

James W. Burgess
Thomas D. Campbell
Almus A. Cane (Bglr)
Asa C. Cane
John C. Carlton
Alexander P. Carter
Richard Carter
James Conover
Henry H. Crocket
Jasper F. Crutchfield
James Curry
William N. Davis (Cpl)
James Denham
Benjamin C. Dent
Henry H. Dent
George W. Dent
John Doles
Cornelius S. Dowd
James D. Eaves
Sterling H. Edmons
James A. Eskridge
Richard W. Eskridge (1 Sgt)
Caleb J. Ethridge
Joseph J. Exum (Com Sgt)
Matthew Exum (Cpl)
Alvin M. Fleming (Sgt)
Josiah H. Foard
Edwin M. Franklin
William N. Galimore
Benjamin F. Galloway
Amos L. Gaskins
Columbus C. Gates
Jesse G. Gibbs
John P. Gibbs (1 Lt)
William H. Gibbs (Com Sgt)
William D. Glasgow
Edward S. Ham
Julius M. Harkey (Cpl)
James Harrington (Cpl)
William J. Hartsfield
James W. Heathcott
Richard Heathcott
Andrew J. Hedgepeth (Sgt)
John E. Hill
Noah H. Hill

William W. Hill
William W. Hubbard
Henry C. Hughes (Cpl)
Joseph D. Hunt
Lewis A. Ivie
John T. Jackson (Sgt)
William A. Jackson
Gideon M. Jolly
Adolphus D. Jones
James N. Julin (2 Lt)
Alfonzo C. Kirk
Hiram W.M. Kirk
James A. Kirk
Lafayette V. Kirk
Joseph L. Lacewell
John R. Lewis (Cpl)
Joel J. Manire
William H. Martin
James R. McElyon
John C. Miller
William A. Molin
James A. Moore
Adam M. Mowery
Simon P. Murphy
John W. Myrick
Brandon C. Ozment
Samuel N. Ozment
Allen W. Parham
James M. Perry
William C. Perry
Daniel E. Phillpott (1 Sgt)
William T. Pointer
Francis M. Prince
Joseph C. Ray
John S. Ray
Robert F. Roberts
Smith A. Roger
John P. Rudd
Andrew D. Saddler
Samuel J. Saddler
Franklin L. Simmons
Lemuel Simmons
William P. Simmons
Henson Smith
William C. Smith

Hiram L. Thomas (Cpl)
William M. Thompson
Robert M. Tribble
John W. Trim
James W. Throgmorton
Joseph Taylor
James M. Trim
James L. Turner
Joseph P. Turner
Frank M. Vermilliom
John R. Waggener (Sgt)
Thomas B. Waggoner (1 Lt)
Issac E. Wainscott (Cpl)
John W. Wainscott
George T. Ware (1 Lt)
Edward J. Wescott (QMS)
Henry H. Williams
James W. Wilson

COMPANY M

Captain
William Carroll Holt

Francis M. Akin (Cpl)
James M. Akin (Cpl)
William P. Baker
Henry J. Benton
James M. Benton
John T. Benton
James H. Black (Cpl)
Lewis Bohannan
William J. Brent
Robert L. Browning
Jesse Butler
Robert K. Canada
John Cantrell
William M. Cantrell
Robert R. Capps
James P. Churchell
Calvin C. Cleaver
Ammens Cochran
John D. Cochran
William G. Corder
John Crafford

April P. Cribbs
James W. Cribbs (Sgt)
William R. Davis
Robert Dawland
James M. Denning (Cpl)
Theopolis Denning
William M. Denning
James G. Elgim
Harvey J. Eskew
Thomas Ezell
Albert R. Flippin (1 Sgt)
James H. Flippin (Sgt)
Robert B. Flowers
John Fox (Cpl)
William Fox
William T. George
John R. Gill
Joseph A. Gray
James F. Hampton
James A. Harrey
John W. Hill
John Hillard
John B. Holt
Michael M. Holt
Thomas E. James
Issac W. Johns
George W. Johnson
Robert E. Jones
William G. Knott
William R. Langley
Joseph W. Lee (Sgt)
Pleasant A. Lee
William D. Leigh
Clark J. Little
William B. Little
Thomas H. Loach
Clem M. Logue
James M. Magnum (2 Lt)
James P. Matthews
James McCarther (Cpl)
Thomas D. McColum
Thad C. McMahan (1 Lt)
Henry J. Meritt
James Mitts
Alex S. Neely

Hugh L. Neely (2 Lt)
William M. Parker
Wesley Parsons
John W. Peevehouse
Lewis Petty
William Powell
Joseph L. Reagan (Sgt)
Barton Reed
Joseph Reynolds
Thomas J. Reynolds
William Reynolds
James H. Ross (1 Sgt)
Joseph G. Sellers
Asher Simpson (Cpl)
Allen D. Smith
John Smith
Zachariah Smith (Cpl)
Richard L. Spear
Joseph R. Thadford (Sgt)
Josias Thadford
James Thedford (Bglr)
Francis A. Tosh
James H. Tosh
John G. Tosh
Riley S. Tosh
Thomas Ward
Zachariah White
Alexander Young
Elbert A. Young
James M. Young
John A. Young

PARTIAL CASUALTY LIST FROM THE ENGAGEMENT NEAR BOLIVAR, TENNESSEE MARCH 29, 1864

The following names were collected from the *Report of the Adjutant General of the State of Tennessee of the Military Forces of the State, from 1861 to 1866* and letters from soldiers of the 6th Tennessee Cavalry contained in the Civil War Collection (IV, K-1, Box 1) at the Tennessee State Library and Archives in Nashville, Tennessee.

Killed

Cpt. John W. Moore (Co. L)
2nd Lt. Hugh L. Neely (Co. M)
Cpl. Thomas Ezell (Co. M)
Pvt. John Connor (Co. B)
Pvt. Green D. Denny (Co. G)
Pvt. Lewis Davis (Co. G)
Pvt. Alexander Earnest (Co. H)

Wounded

Sgt. Reuben H. Beazley (Co. K)
Pvt. Henry H. Dent (Co. L)
Pvt. John F. Allman (Co. I)
Pvt. Pink Lee (Co. I)
Pvt. Coleman D. Smith (Co. I)

Captured

Cpt. William C. Holt (Co. M)
Sgt. Reuben H. Beazley (Co. K)
Cpl. James B. Thacker (Co. B)
Pvt. William Baker (Co. M)
Pvt. James Crebbs (Co. M)
Pvt. Harve Esque (Co. M)
Pvt. James A. Harvey (Co. M)

Pvt. John R. Henderson (Co. B)
Pvt. Thomas Leach (Co. M)
Pvt. William B. Little (Co. M)
Pvt. James P. Mathis (Co. K)
Pvt. William B. May (Co. H)
Pvt. John W. Peevehouse (M)
Pvt. Allen D. Smith (Co. M)
Pvt. William J. Stafford (Co. K)
Pvt. James M. Young (Co. M)

Missing in Action

Pvt. James M. Steel (Co. I)

BIOGRAPHICAL SKETCHES OF OFFICERS IN THE 6TH TENNESSEE CAVALRY

Dr. Job Bell (1826-1904)

Dr. Job Bell was born on July 26, 1826 in McNairy County, Tennessee. He became a physician as early as 1849, serving as the family doctor of Fielding Hurst. On October 12, 1863 Hurst appointed him as the 2nd Assistant Surgeon for the 6th Tennessee Cavalry with the rank of lieutenant, a position he would hold until his resignation on March 3, 1865.

After the war, Dr. Bell returned to his medical practice in McNairy County. He was also elected county court clerk, serving from 1878 to 1882. He later moved to Henderson, Tennessee where he died on February 25, 1904 at the age of 80. He was buried at Mt. Gilead Cemetery in northwest McNairy County. The epitaph on his large tombstone described him as "Physician, Soldier & Gentleman." [1]

Thomas H. Boswell (b. circa 1833)

Thomas H. Boswell was born in Wilson County, Tennessee about 1833. He was a merchant when the war began. He enlisted in Company D of the 1st West Tennessee Infantry as a 1st lieutenant at Dresden, Tennessee on July 15, 1862. Company D consisted of men from Weakley County. He quickly rose to captain on August 9, 1862.

---

[1] *McNairy County Independent*, February 26, 1904; Job Bell Military Services Records (TSLA); Melocky Hurst Widow Pension Application (NA); Job Bell tombstone at Mt. Gilead Cemetery, McNairy County, Tennessee.

When the 1st West Tennessee Infantry consolidated into the 6th Tennessee Cavalry, Boswell was elevated to the rank of major on July 1, 1863. During a skirmish at Salem, Mississippi, he was wounded in the right shoulder, the effects of which remained with him the remainder of his military service. As a result, much of this period was spent at military hospitals in Tennessee and at Paducah, Kentucky.

Boswell submitted his resignation as major on June 28, 1864, still suffering from the effects of his wound. It rendered him, according to regimental surgeon Thomas Williams, "entirely unfit for either Invalid Corps or Field service, and [he] will not, during his term of service, recover sufficiently to resume his duties." His resignation was accepted on October 26, 1864.[2]

Churchill E. Bondurant (b. circa 1841)

Churchill E. Bondurant was born in Weakley County, Tennessee. A schoolteacher before the war, he enlisted in the 1st West Tennessee Infantry at Dresden, Tennessee. He was promoted to sergeant major in the 6th Tennessee Cavalry on August 1, 1864. He later became a hospital steward on May 25, 1865.[3]

William K.M. Breckenridge (1825-1863)

William K.M. Breckenridge lived in Wayne County, Tennessee when the war began. He was appointed lieutenant colonel of the 1st West Tennessee (later 6th Tennessee) Cavalry by Colonel Fielding Hurst on November 13, 1862. He would often serve as regimental commander in Hurst's absence. In March 1863, he was placed under military arrest for unspecified reasons. He died at Grand Junction, Tennessee from an unspecified disease on October 15, 1863. His remains were initially buried at Saltillo, Tennessee but were later interred at the Shiloh National Cemetery in Section C, Grave Number 2219.[4]

William Chandler (circa 1834-1910)

William Chandler was married to Narcissa Moore, niece of Colonel Fielding Hurst by his sister Martha (Hurst) Moore. He enlisted in the 1st

---

[2] Thomas H. Boswell Military Service Records (TSLA); 1860 Census for Weakley County, Tennessee.
[3] Churchill E. Bondurant Military Service Records (TSLA).
[4] William K.M. Breckenridge Military Service Records (TSLA); Shiloh National Cemetery website <www.shilohbattlefield.org/cemetery/detail1.asp?GRAVE=C-2219>

West Tennessee Cavalry on September 20, 1862. He became captain of Company G and proved to be troublesome during his service. He was arrested on October 3, 1863 for being absent with his command without orders. He was later dismissed from military service on November 19, 1864. Even after his dismissal, it was discovered that he had been "levying contributions upon the citizens of McNairy County, Tenn., to the amount of $50,000." He died at Unionville, Illinois on April 13, 1910.[5]

Risden Davis Deford (1839-1919)

Risden Davis Deford was born in Alleghany City, Pennsylvania on September 28, 1839. He relocated with his family to Lauderdale County, Alabama before the war. Their anti-slavery sentiments were not welcomed as three secessionists attacked him on a Florence, Alabama street and would have killed him had not a passerby intervened.

While his father decided to go north with his family to Illinois, Risden Deford and his brothers chose to stay and fight. After relocating across the state line to Hardin County, Tennessee, he joined Company H of the 1st West Tennessee Cavalry at Bolivar, Tennessee on December 20, 1862 with the rank of 1st lieutenant. When Captain Joseph G. Berry was discharged from military service, he was promoted to succeed him on October 7, 1864. Deford was severely wounded during a skirmish at Salem, Mississippi on October 7, 1863. During the battle, he led a battalion of the 6th Tennessee Cavalry and "earned the praise of his superior officers."

After the war, Deford returned to Hardin County and with his brother Harve went into business at Cerro Gordo. He later invested in a mill on Indian Creek at Olive Hill, Tennessee in 1886. He served for two years in the state legislature representing Hardin County as a member of the Republican Party (1901-1903). His son James Edward Deford would later serve in the same office.

Risden D. Deford died on November 12, 1911 at Savannah, Tennessee. He was buried at the City Cemetery in Savannah.[6]

---

[5] William Chandler Military Service Records (TSLA); *O.R.* I, 49, part 2: 751.
[6] Risden D. Deford Military Service Records (TSLA); Andrew P. Hitt, *Short Life Sketches of Some Prominent Hardin* Countians: ; Wade Pruitt, *Bugger Saga: The Civil War Story of Guerrilla and Bushwhacker Warfare in Lauderdale County, Alabama and Southern Middle Tennessee*: 57-58.

Daniel M. Emerson

Daniel M. Emerson became major of the 2nd Battalion of the 1st West Tennessee Cavalry (later 6th Tennessee) upon the recommendation of Brigadier General Mason Brayman. He was a Northerner but his military records did not specify his residence at the time of the war.

Emerson was pressured to resign, however, as he had been "appointed…against the wishes of the officers & men" under his command. He felt to "do them Justice [sic]" it was "absolutely necessary…to resign my position, & enter the service elsewhere." His resignation was accepted on July 13, 1863. Major General Richard Oglesby noted on the back of his letter of resignation that Emerson had been placed in a regiment "he had nothing on earth to do with raising or organizing."[7]

Richard W. Eskridge (b. circa 1843)

Richard W. Eskridge was born in Weakley County, Tennessee and enlisted in the 1st West Tennessee Infantry at Dresden on July 4, 1862. He was promoted to 1st sergeant on November 21, 1862. He was transferred to Company B and became its 2nd lieutenant on September 17, 1864. He became the regimental commissary of subsistence on March 28, 1865.[8]

Elijah James Hodges (1831-1913)

Elijah James Hodges was born in McNairy County, Tennessee on May 18, 1831. He and his brother Horry enlisted in Company B of the 1st West Tennessee Cavalry at Bethel Station on August 25, 1862. He stood exceptionally tall for a man of the era at an impressive six feet and six inches tall. On November 17, he was promoted to sergeant and on October 16, 1863, he was elevated to adjutant. Upon the death of his brother Harry Hodges, Elijah replaced him as captain of Company B on February 29, 1864.

After the war, Hodges was elected to the Tennessee General Assembly for one term representing McNairy County (1867-1869). In 1880, he became a minister in the Primitive Baptist denomination and served the remainder of his life. "He was a great literary as well as Bible reader," his obituary published in the McNairy County *Independent* stated. "In his blind-

---

[7] Daniel M. Emerson Military Service Record (TSLA).

[8] Richard W. Eskridge Military Service Records (TSLA).

ness [contracted a year before his death] a day never passed that he was not read to by members of his family." Hodges died at his home two miles east of McNairy on April 21, 1913. He was laid to rest at Mount Carmel Cemetery in Finger, Tennessee.[9]

William Carroll Holt (1845-1917)

A resident of Bloomfield, Missouri before the war, William Carroll Holt enlisted in Company E of the 1st West Tennessee Infantry on July 18, 1862. When the regiment was consolidated to form the 6th Tennessee Cavalry, he was promoted to captain of Company M in the new command.

He was captured during the battle at Bolivar, Tennessee on March 29, 1864 and taken prisoner to Andersonville, Georgia for a short time before being moved to other Confederate prisons at Macon and Savannah, Georgia and Charleston and Columbia, South Carolina. For two to three months, he suffered from "chronic diarrhea brought on by exposure" and was hospitalized. While imprisoned at Columbia, he escaped on foot and made his way back to the 6th Tennessee. He traveled only under the cover of darkness and eventually rejoined his company around March 11, 1865.

The ordeal rendered him ineffective for military service the remainder of the war. He died at Dresden, Tennessee in 1917 and was buried at Sunset Cemetery in Dresden.[10]

Levi Hurst (1809-1887)

Levi Hurst was a fifty-one-year-old tenant farmer who lived near the Monterey community in McNairy County, Tennessee when the war began. He was not related to Colonel Fielding Hurst and his family. Prior to the war, he had lived in Wayne County where he was the sheriff in the early 1840s and was a minister in the Primitive Baptist Church.

Hurst's sons were divided by the war, his four youngest ones serving with him in the 6th Tennessee Cavalry and his two older ones in the Confederacy. He enlisted in the 1st West Tennessee Cavalry on September 12,

---

[9] Elijah James Hodges Military Service Records (TSLA); John E. Talbott J.D., *Let's Call It Finger!* : 75; McNairy County Independent, April 25, 1913; Robert M. McBride and Dan M. Robison, eds. *Biographical Directory of the Tennessee General Assembly*. Vol. 2: 423-424.

[10] William Carroll Holt Military Service Records (TSLA); James Buckley Chapter, NSDAR, comp. *Weakley County, Tennessee Cemetery Listings*. 301. Jack Darrel Wood correspondence, 26 Dec. 2007.

1862 and was elected the first captain of Company D. He was honorably discharged on June 29, 1864 after it was determined he was too ill from heart palpitations and hemorrhoids to serve. He applied for a pension, but he was unable to prove to the Federal Government that his disability resulted from his military service.[11]

Nathan McDonald Kemp (1830-1912)

Nathan McDonald Kemp was born on June 8, 1830 "on the head waters of Snake Creek" in McNairy County, Tennessee. "Mack" was deputy sheriff of Hardin County when the war began. He enlisted in Company C of the 6th Tennessee Cavalry on September 11, 1862 and was elected captain, serving in that capacity throughout the war.

When the war ended, Tennessee Governor William G. Brownlow appointed Kemp sheriff of Hardin County in 1865. He later served as commander of the Grand Army of the Republic (GAR) Post 7 in Adamsville, Tennessee. He died on December 4, 1912 and was buried at Shiloh National Cemetery in Section R, Grave 3613.[12]

Samuel Lewis (1826-1867)

Samuel Lewis was born in McNairy County, Tennessee circa 1826. At the age of thirty-six, he enlisted as a private in Company A of the 1st West Tennessee Cavalry at Bethel Station on August 11, 1862. He was promoted to 1st sergeant on October 1, 1862 and 2nd lieutenant on December 15. The company muster roll noted that he had deserted at Bolivar, Tennessee but returned seven days later. When James J. Smith became chaplain for the regiment, Lewis replaced him as 1st lieutenant. He became captain of Company A on November 21, 1864, but he was forced to resign after suffering six months with a condition described as "pericardial dropsy." His resignation was accepted on June 3, 1865.

Lewis was appointed the ninth sheriff of McNairy County and took office on August 1, 1865. He was re-elected two years later. While trying to calm a

[11] Levi Hurst Military Service Records (TSLA); Levi Hurst Military Pension Application (courtesy of Marilyn Rushing).

[12] Nathan McDonald Kemp Military Service Records (TSLA). Clifton (TN) *Mirror*, June 16, 1905. "Newspaper Article: Nathan McDonald Kemp." Kemp Family Chronicles. Jeff Kemp. October 25, 2006 <http://www.kempchronicles.com/doc.html>. Shiloh National Cemetery. Shiloh National Military Park. October 25, 2006. <www.shilohbattlefield.org/cemetery/choice.asp>.

group of African-American soldiers that were harassing a freedman in Purdy, Tennessee, he was shot and mortally wounded by one of the soldiers on July 27, 1867. He was buried at Buena Vista Cemetery in McNairy County.[13]

Orlando H. Shearer (b. circa 1830 or 1835)

A twenty-five-year-old saloonkeeper from Havana, Mason County, Illinois, Orlando Shearer enlisted in the 1st Tennessee Infantry on June 20, 1862 and was elected 1st lieutenant. He was promoted to captain of Company I on September 25, 1862. On October 16, 1863 he was elevated to major in the 6th Tennessee Cavalry and lieutenant colonel on March 20, 1865 when William J. Smith was promoted to colonel. Based on his "gallant and meritious service" during the war, Shearer attained the rank of brevet colonel on October 14, 1865. During the absence of Colonel Biddle in April 1865, he was placed in command of the 2nd Brigade of the 6th Division Cavalry Corps, Military Division of the Mississippi. After the war, Shearer returned to being a saloonkeeper in Havana, Illinois.[14]

Robert M. Thompson (1830-1903)

Robert M. Thompson was born in North Carolina. He was a merchant, preacher, and postmaster in Purdy, Tennessee before the war began. He enlisted in Company A and became its first captain in August 1862.

He served as a recruiter for Military Governor Andrew Johnson, a service that Colonel Fielding Hurst disagreed with as it took him away from the regiment for extended periods of time. The February 1864 muster roll for the 6th Tennessee Cavalry listed him as absent without leave and his pay was suspended. Hurst wanted Thompson to return to the regiment, claiming he had "been attempting to recruit for nearly six months without accomplishing anything what[so]ever."

Still considered absent without leave, Thompson wrote to Assistant Adjutant General William H. Morgan on November 12, 1864 and explained that he had been authorized by Governor Johnson to recruit for an infantry

---

[13] Samuel Lewis Military Service Records (TSLA); Bolivar (TN) *Bulletin*, August 3, 1867 (courtesy of Carrie Bergquist).

[14] 1860 and 1870 Census for Mason County, Illinois; Orlando H. Shearer Military Service Records (TSLA).

regiment with permission from 16th Army Corps commander Cadwallader C. Washburn. A requisition note dated July 18, 1864 stated that Thompson was traveling from Cairo, Illinois to Paducah, Kentucky "recruiting per order of Gov. Johnson approved by Maj. Gen. Washburn May 16, 1864." Nevertheless, Washburn rescinded his approval and ordered Thompson back to his regiment.

Thompson resigned as major of the 6th Tennessee and recruiter for the 11th Tennessee Infantry on October 26, 1864, stating that he needed to care for his wife and children as well as his elderly parents. They had been forced to leave McNairy County because of "numerous outrages committed upon them by the Rebels [*sic*]" and were living in Paducah. Another reason was medical in nature, a groin injury that prohibited him from riding a horse.

After the war, Thompson returned to McNairy County and resumed his pastoral work, bringing the Wesleyan Methodist anti-slavery denomination to the region. He also tried unsuccessfully to revive higher education in the county through Purdy College, which had been abandoned during the war. He also served as McNairy County court clerk (1866-1870).[15] When Congress enacted the Southern Claims Commission in 1872, Thompson represented several applicants in McNairy and surrounding counties and worked to help them secure reimbursement for property losses during the war.[16]

In May 1886, Thompson was charged with withholding pension money from the minor heirs of Thomas McCall for whom he served as guardian. He fled before a sentence was handed down in court, however, and for the next two years he engaged in various business pursuits in Washington D.C. and New York. He was apprehended two years later while making his way back south selling stock in Idaho silver mines.[17]

Stanford L. Warren (1837-1883)

Stanford L. Warren was born in McNairy County, Tennessee, the son of James and Louisa (Raine) Warren. Before the war, he practiced law in Purdy and was co-publisher of the *West Tennessee Argus* newspaper. He enlisted in the 1st West Tennessee Cavalry at Bethel Station on September 15, 1862

---

[15] Robert M. Thompson Military Service Records (TSLA); Graf and Haskins, eds. *The Papers of Andrew Johnson*. 6:686; Wright, *Reminiscences*. 83.
[16] Southern Claims Commission (see Sources for complete listing).
[17] "An Alleged Pension Swindler." Washington *Post*, 5 May 1888. ProQuest Historical Newspapers.

and was made 1st lieutenant and adjutant by Colonel Fielding Hurst. He was mustered into service at LaGrange, Tennessee on July 1, 1863. His servant, Anderson, accompanied him throughout the war.

Warren was promoted to captain of Company I on October 16, 1863 and became a major on March 28, 1865. During the latter part of the war, he was elected to the 35th Tennessee General Assembly representing McNairy County for one term and took an extended leave of absence from the regiment to attend.

President Andrew Johnson appointed him to be the U.S. District Attorney for West Tennessee (1867-1868). He returned to politics and was elected as a state representative to the 36th General Assembly (1869-1871) and a state senator in the 37th and 38th General Assemblies (1871-1875).[18]

---

[18] Stanford L. Warren Military Service Records (TSLA); McBride and Robison, eds. *Biographical Directory*: 954-955; Wright, *Reminiscences*: 83.

SAMUEL M. MEEK LETTER
DECEMBER 4, 1861

Captain Samuel Mills Meek was a member of Company H in the 35th Mississippi Infantry, which was assigned to escort several Unionist prisoners (including Fielding Hurst) to the train station at Corinth, Mississippi. This is a letter he wrote home that describes what happened. The transcription includes spelling and grammatical errors contained in the original letter. It is owned by Colleen Holland and has been printed with her permission.

"Camp Davis" Corinth Missi.
Dec 4th 1861 - 8 oclock P.M.

My own dearest Lou,

We have just gotten through with the duties of the day—stationed the Guard for the night; and while the boys are "turning in" for the night, I cannot close my eyes without saying a word to her, who is dearest to my heart, than the "apple of my eye"—in fact, who is as essential to my happiness as atmosphere, is to the healthy condition of the lungs—or religion to the soul of the sinner. There is not a moment my dearest Lou, that your image is not before my eyes, indelibly imprinted as it is upon the inmost walls of my heart—all the dear ones at home—Mother—Sister—brothers, wife and little boy—constitute the food for thought, and the images for dreams. But enough for this. You all know how dear you are to me, and how I love you. Is it not a weakness my dear, to love so much If so, it is a weakness, for which I thank my God.

I wrote you a short note today, and I now have no news—but a few incidents of camp life and soldierly duty, I will give you.

Today I received orders from "Head Quarters" to detail ten men a Sergeant & Corporal and march to the Court-House to Guard six "Lincolns" Prisoners, who were arrested by a Company sent from this place, into Mc Nairy Co. Tennessee which is the adjoining County. They were arrested about twenty miles from this place. One of them, the ring-leader, a man name Sanders escaped. The Company surrounded his house, at night, and he fired upon them from the window - they returned the fire—and in the confusion of the moment, he escaped. However they succeeded in capturing three of his sons. One of the Prisoners Fielding Hurst is a man of wealth and position in his county—a lawyer of good standing in his profession and a very intelligent, shrewd fellow—Another, is a Preacher, J. P. Prince said to be of the Campbellite persuation—the others farmers—We began our duty at 10 oclock, in the morning, and at 1 oclock, we were ordered to conduct them to the Rail Road, where they were placed under the control of the "Confederate States Martial, for the middle District of Tennessee," with a squad of soldiers, who started with them to Nashville to be indicted and tried for Treason. I conversed with them freely, and they some what excited my sympathies, as they talked of their families at home, but if they are guilty, they do not deserve the communication of any human beings.

As we marched them through the streets—to the R. Road, we were surrounded by a dense crowd, of excited, curious people, all anxious to get a sight of the "infernal Lincanites" as they called them. It was truly an awful sight to see men, born upon Southern soil, compelled to be marched like felons through the streets, of a town not 20 miles from their residence, charged with <u>Treason</u> to their State and their Section. They should be speedily and promptly dealt with. So you see, we have done already, work, more pleasant than <u>digging ditches</u>!

We are encamped, on a beautiful knoll, in the northern part of the town - with other companies all around us. The camp fires—dotting the entire hill and white tents visible under the clear starlight, presents a most picturesque appearance.

When our Regt' is formed we will be ordered to Columbus Ky to take possession of a fort. So says Genl' Davis.

Bro. Roger, with a small squad is encamped about 50 yds from us. They are trying to get up a Company from thier own County—They may join us yet—not by any means certain—

Fife not dead yet, but our boys, almost with womans tenderness, watch the stars out by the bed of vain. The Or's think he will die tonight. He is at the hotel.

Don't forget, always & ever, to give my love to Miss Betty (may I dearest?) She is so good, and kind & true a friend that she is almost like my own Sister—I will write to her soon.

My hoarseness, is gradually giving way - I feel well—My love to Muddie—Sue, Emmons—Arny—and my darling little Willie—Remind him of his Pa—every day—

My letters are only for home folks—you know—

Good night my dearest Lou—May the God of all things protect you & I and all of us from harm and bring us soon again, together—I find friends here – "hearts devoid of guile, find friends where ever they go"—

Write often—Good Night—God bless you all—

Your own devoted—S. M. Meek

to Mrs. S. M. Meek

I have not a line from home yet—Look for a letter tomorrow—Will I get it?—

Address your letters to "S. M. Meek—Care of Capt Brown—Capt of Reuben Davis Rifles, Corinth Missi"

Dec. 5—

I feel well this morning—Fife—poor old man died last night, and we send two men—Powell & Lawrence home with him. They will return—next Thursday—His wife is at Mr Rose's I suppose you can find out his movements from him—

Send me by him, if possible, a Blanket <u>jacket</u>, to come just below the hips—Frazer will cut it out—He has my measures. If you can't get Blanket—then some other coarse warm cloth—with this or a coarse heavy <u>over shirt</u> made soldier fashion—

Good by—I will write to your Ma—next time—I have heard not a word from Louis yet—Do all write— a letter every other day at least—

S. M - M

BIBLIOGRAPHY

Key

JMCL   Jackson-Madison County Library (Jackson, TN)
LC   Library of Congress (Washington D.C.)
NA   National Archives (Washington D.C.)
SCC   Southern Claims Commission (www.footnote.com)
THQ   Tennessee Historical Quarterly
TSLA   Tennessee State Library and Archives (Nashville, TN)
WTHSP   West Tennessee Historical Society Papers

Manuscripts and Letters

Bills, John Houston Diary at TSLA.
Brownlow, William G. Governors Papers at TSLA
Chiers, Nathaniel. "Personal Experiences in the Civil War." Civil War
     Collection, Account 1252, Box 1, Folder 5 at TSLA.
Chester, Mary to William Butler Chester, February 18, 1864. Manuscript
     Division, Account 68-287 at TSLA.
Denham, James to J.F. Denham, April 7, 1864. Civil War Collection,
     Account 68-287 at TSLA.
Field and Staff Muster Roll of the 6th Tennessee (Union) Cavalry at NA.
     (Photocopies courtesy of Jack Darrel Wood at JMCL.)
Hurst, Fielding Adoption Appeal. McNairy County Chancery Court Min-
     utes, October 16, 1868 on microfilm at TSLA.
Hurst, Fielding to Samuel R. Rodgers, July 27, 1865. Box 2, Folder 11, Item
     18. O.P. Temple Papers. Special Collections Library at Hoskins Library,
     University of Tennessee Knoxville.
Johnson, Andrew Papers. LC (on microfilm at TSLA).
Johnson, Andrew Military Governor Papers at TSLA.
Johnson, Andrew Miscellaneous Papers, Account 124 at TSLA.
Knotts, Harvey to L.B. Knotts, June 29, 1865. Manuscript Division, Ac-
     count 68-287 at TSLA.
Lawrence, Henry to William Lawrence, April 5, 1864. Manuscript Division,
     Account 68-287 at TSLA.
Lawrence, Henry to Dr. C. Revis, April 5, 1864. Manuscript Division,
     Account 68-287 at TSLA.

Parker, William M. Civil War Questionnaire at TSLA.

Regimental Letter Book and Regimental Order Book of the 6th Tennessee (Union) Cavalry at NA. (Photocopies courtesy of Jack Darrel Wood at JMCL.)

Robertson, Christopher W. Civil War Questionnaire at TSLA.

Tennessee Adjutant General Records. Manuscript Division at TSLA.

Union Provost Marshal's Papers Relating to Individual Citizens at TSLA.

Wisdom, Dew M. to Col. Philip D. Roddey, July 23, 1863. NARA M474, RG 109, Reel 88, Frames 167-169 at NA.

Wright, Marcus J. Diary (April 23, 1861 to February 26, 1863). Civil War Collection, Box 7, Folder 5 at TSLA.

Individual Military Service Records at the National Archives (Washington D.C.)

Bell, Job
Boswell, Thomas H.
Bondurant, Churchill E.
Breckenridge, William K.M.
Chandler, William
DeFord, Risden D.
Emerson, Daniel M.
Hodges, Elijah J.
Holt, William Carroll
Hurst, Fielding
Hurst, Levi
Lewis, Samuel
Little, William B.
Plunk, John Wesley
Shearer, Orlando H.
Smith, William J.
Thompson, Robert M.
Warren, Stanford L.

Southern Claims Commission (www.footnote.com)

Cheshier, Pitser M. (No. 17782)
Hughes, William C. (No. 17798)
King, Jackson J. (No. 17806)
Simms, William and L.Y. Bledsoe (No. 1507)

Official Documents

Acts of the General Assembly of the State of Tennessee Passed at the First Session of the Thirty-Fourth General Assembly for the Year 1865. Nashville, TN: S.C. Mercer, 1865.

McNairy County, Tennessee Circuit Court Minutes, Book B.

Report of the Adjutant General of the State of Tennessee of the Military Forces of the State from 1861 to 1866. Nashville, TN: S.C. Mercer, 1866.

Senate Journal of the First Session of the General Assembly of the State of Tennessee, 1865. Nashville, TN: S.C. Mercer, 1865.

U.S. War Department. *The War of the Rebellion: A Compilation of the Official Records of the Union and Confederate Armies.* Washington D.C.: Government Printing Office, 1889. Series I, 53 volumes.

Newspapers

Jackson *Sun* (Jackson, Tennessee)
Memphis *Bulletin* (Memphis, Tennessee)
Memphis *Commercial-Appeal* (Memphis, Tennessee)
Memphis *Press-Scimitar* (Memphis, Tennessee)
McNairy County *Independent* (Selmer, Tennessee)
Nashville *Union and American* (Nashville, Tennessee)
New York *Times* (New York, New York)
Richmond *Daily Dispatch* (Richmond, Virginia)

Electronic Documents and Internet Websites

Ambrose, Stephen. "Remembering Sultana." National Geographic. (May 1, 2001) August 11, 2007 <news.nationalgeographic.com/news/2001/05/0501_river5.html>

Brown, Andrew. "Sol Street, Confederate Partisan Leader." *Journal of Mississippi History.* 21.6 (1959) August 8, 2007 <www.rootsweb.com/~mscivilw/solstreet.htm>

Civil War Soldiers and Sailors System. National Park Service. November 7, 2006. <www.itd.nps.gov/cwss/index.html>

Davis, Judge Orlando. Diary. <www.rootsweb.com/%7emscivilw/davis.htm>

Holmes, Annie Cole. "War Leaflets." Charles Holmes, contributor. November 7, 2006. www.rootsweb.com/~tncarroll/civilwar/warleaflets.htm

Lockhart Tommy, Bill Gurney, and W. Fred Cox. "1860 Census of Tippah County, Mississippi." July 12, 2007. <www.rootsweb.com/~mstippah/1860-s.html>

Tennessee Civil War Sourcebook. James B. Jones Jr., editor. November 7, 2006. <www.tennesseecivilwarsourcebook.com>

The War of the Rebellion: A Compilation of the Official Records of the Union and Confederate Armies. Cornell University. 7 November 2006 <http://0-cdl.library.cornell.edu.source.unco.edu/moa/browse.monographs/waro.html>

Articles

"Gen. Forrest Among Civilians." *Confederate Veteran* 3.4 (April 1895).

Alderson, William T., ed. "The Civil War Reminiscences of John Johnston." *THQ* 13:3 (September 1954).

Bates, Walter Lynn. "Southern Unionists: A Socio-Economic Examination of the Third East Tennessee Volunteer Infantry Regiment U.S.A." *THQ* 50.4 (Winter 1991).

Blair, Dale. "Heard Roar of Shiloh Guns as Boy Slave, Negro Claims." Memphis *Commercial-Appeal*, September 3, 1963.

Blankenship, Gary R. "Colonel Fielding Hurst and the Hurst Nation." *WTHSP* 34 (October 1980).

Fisher, Noel C. "'Prepare Them For My Coming': General William T. Sherman, Total War, and Pacification in West Tennessee." *THQ* 51:2.

Green, J.U. "Prison Life and Escape of Col. J.U. Green." *Confederate Veteran* 7:1 (January 1899).

Lapides, George. "Story of Col. Hurst, the Fearless Yankee." Memphis *Press-Scimitar*, February 19, 1963.

Lufkin, Charles L. "Divided Loyalties: Sectionalism in Civil War McNairy County." *THQ* 47 (Fall 1988).

Potter, Jerry O'Neil. "The First West Tennessee Raid of General Nathan Bedford Forrest." *WTHSP* 28 (1974).

Reed, Mary S. "The Family Hurst: An Absorbing History." Jackson *Sun*, February 20, 1983.

Williams, Emma Inman, ed. "Hettie Wisdom Tapp's Memoirs." *WTHSP* 36 (1982).

Theses and Dissertations

Blankenship, Gary R. "Fielding Hurst, Tennessee Tory: A Study of a West Tennessee Unionist of the American Civil War." Master's thesis, Memphis State University, 1977.

Frisby, Derek William. "'Homemade Yankees': West Tennessee Unionism in the Civil War Era." Doctoral dissertation, University of Alabama, 2004.

Books

A Member of the G.A.R. *The Picket Line and Camp Fire Stories; A Collection of War Anecdotes, Both Grave and Gray.* New York: Hurst and Company, n.d.

Alexander, Thomas B. *Political Reconstruction in Tennessee.* Nashville, TN: Vanderbilt University Press, 1950.

Atwater, Dorance, comp. *Atwater Report: List of Prisoners Who Died in 1864-65 at Andersonville Prison.* Andersonville, GA: National Society of Andersonville, 1885.

Bergeron, Paul H. *Paths of the Past: Tennessee, 1770-1970.* Knoxville, TN: University of Tennessee Press, 1979.

Branch, Virginia. *The Hurst Nation: A Family History.* Paragould, AR: self-published, 1987.

Civil War Centennial Commission. *Tennesseans in the Civil War: A Military History of Confederate and Union Units with Available Rosters of Personnel.* Nashville, TN: Civil War Centennial Commission, 1964-65. 2 volumes.

Coffin, Charles Carleton. *My Days and Nights on the Battlefield.* Boston, MA: Dana Estes and Company, 1887.

Corlew, Robert E. *Tennessee, A Short History.* Knoxville: University of Tennessee Press, 1990.

Cottrell, Steve. *Civil War in Tennessee.* Gretna, LA: Pelican Publishing Company, 2001.

Coulter, E. Merton. *William G. Brownlow: Fighting Parson of the Southern Highlands.* Knoxville, TN: University of Tennessee Press, 1971.

Croft, Daniel W. *Reluctant Confederates: Upper South Unionists in the Secession Crisis.* Chapel Hill, NC: University of North Carolina Press, 1989.

Current, Richard Nelson. *Lincoln's Loyalists: Union Soldiers from the Confederacy.* New York: Oxford University Press, 1992.

Davis, Burke. *Sherman's March.* New York: Vintage Books, 1988.

Elliott, Colleen Morse and Louise Armstrong Moxley, eds. *Tennessee Civil War Veteran Questionnaires.* Easley, SC: Southern Historical Press, 1985.

Fletcher, Andrew J. and J.O. Shackleford. *The Republican Party in Tennessee Reorganized.* No publisher, 1870.

Garrett, Jill, ed. *Obituaries from Tennessee Newspapers.* Easley, SC: Southern Historical Press, 1980.

Graf, Leroy and Ralph W. Haskins, eds. *The Papers of Andrew Johnson.* Knoxville, TN: University of Tennessee Press, 1979. Volumes 5-6.

Grimsley, Mark. *The Hard Hand of War: Union Military Policy Toward Southern Civilians, 1861-1865.* Cambridge, MA: Cambridge University Press, 1995.

Hallum, John. *Reminiscences of the Civil War.* Little Rock, AR: Tunnah and Pittard, 1903.

Halphin, T.E., ed. *Memphis City Directory 1866.* Memphis, TN: Bingham, Williams & Company, 1866.

Harris, William C. *With Charity for All: Lincoln and the Restoration of the Union.* Lexingtion, KY: University Press of Kentucky, 1999.

Hitt, Andrew P. *Short Life Sketches of Some Prominent Hardin Countians.* Savannah, TN: Custom Productions, n.d.

Hubbard, John Milton. *Notes of a Private.* Memphis, TN: E.H. Clarke & Brother, 1909.

Hurst, Jack. *Nathan Bedford Forrest, a Biography.* New York: Alfred A. Knopf, 1993.

Jones, Wilmer L., Ph.D. *Behind Enemy Lines: Civil War Spies, Raiders, and Guerrillas.* Dallas, TX: Taylor Publishing Company, 2001.

Jordan, Thomas and J.P. Pryor. *The Campaigns of Lieut.-Gen. N.B. Forrest and of Forrest's Cavalry.* Dayton, OH: Press of Morningside Bookshop, 1973.

Kirkland, Frazar. *The Pictorial Book of Anecdotes and Incidents of the War of the Rebellion, Civil, Military, Naval, and Domestic.* Hartford, CT: Hartford Publishing Company, 1867.

Langsdon, Phillip. *Tennessee: A Political History.* Franklin, TN: Hillsboro Press, 2000.

Marszalek, John F. *Sherman: A Soldier's Passion for Order.* New York: The Free Press, 1993.

McBride, Robert M. and Dan M. Robison, eds. *Biographical Direectory of the Tennessee General Assembly: Vol. II, 1861-1901.* Nashville, TN: Tennessee State Library and Archives and Tennessee Historical Commission, 1979.

Mitchell, Frank. *The Hurst Nation and Its People.* Selmer, TN: G & P Printing Services, 2003.

Perkins, Jacob R. Trails, *Rails and War: The Life of Gen. G.M. Dodge.* Indianapolis, IN: Bobbs-Merrill Company, 1929.

Pitts, John A. *Personal and Professional Reminiscences of an Old Lawyer.* Kingsport, TN: Southern Publishers, 1930.

Pruitt, Wade. *Bugger Saga: The Civil War Story of Guerrilla and Bushwhacker Warfare in Lauderdale County, Alabama and Southern Middle Tennessee.* Columbia, TN: P-Vine Press, 1977.

Reflections Committee for the Tennessee 200 Bicentennial Celebration, ed. *Reflections: A History of McNairy County, Tennessee, 1823-1996.* Marceline, MO: Heritage House Publishing, 1996.

Roland, Charles P. *Albert Sidney Johnston: Soldier of Three Republics.* Austin, TX: University of Texas Press, 1990.

Simon, John ed. *The Papers of Ulysses S. Grant.* Carbondale, IL: Southern Illinois Press, 1973. Volume 5.

Stampp, Kenneth M. *The Era of Reconstruction, 1865-1877.* New York: Vintage Books, 1965.

Talbott, John E. J.D. *Let's Call It Finger! A History of North McNairy County and Finger, Tennessee and Its Surrounding Communities.* Self-published, 2003.

Wagoner, Bill. *Shiloh Remembered: A Collection of Bill Wagoner's Wagon Spokes.* Savannah, TN: Banner Publishing Company, 1987.

Warner, Ezra. *Generals in Blue: Lives of the Union Commanders.* Baton Rogue, LA: Louisiana State University Press, 1964.

Williams, Emma Inman. *Historic Madison: The Story of Jackson and Madison County, Tennessee from the Prehistoric Moundbuilders to 1917.* Jackson, TN: Madison County Historical Society, 1946.

Willis, Brian Steel. *A Battle from the Start: The Life of Nathan Bedford Forrest.* New York: HarperCollins, 1992.

Wyeth, John Allan. *That Devil Forrest: Life of General Nathan Bedford Forrest.* Baton Rogue: Louisiana State University Press, 1989.

INDEX

1

12th Tennessee (C.S.), 72
12th Tennessee Cavalry (C.S.), 31
13th Tennessee Cavalry (U.S.), 77
14th Tennessee (C.S.), 72
15th Tennessee (C.S.), 72
15th Tennessee Cavalry (C.S.), 34
16th Army Corps (U.S.), 45, 48, 64, 66,
    68, 70, 76, 78, 80, 125
18th Illinois Mounted Infantry, 31
19th Pennsylvania Cavalry, 78
1st West Tennessee Infantry (U.S.), 44

2

2nd Cavalry Brigade (U.S.), 37
2nd Iowa Cavalry, 37, 40
2nd Iowa Cavalry (U.S.), 37, 40
2nd Mississippi Cavalry, 28
2nd New Jersey Cavalry, 78
2nd West Tennessee Cavalry. See 7th
    Tennessee Cavalry (U.S.)

3

35th MS Infantry (C.S.), 11
3rd Illinois Cavalry, 46
3rd Michigan Cavalry, 37, 40, 47
3rd Michigan Cavalry (U.S.), 40

4

43rd Illinois Infantry, 22
48th Illinois Cavalry, 18
4th Illinois Cavalry, 81
4th Missouri Cavalry (U.S.), 78

6

61st Illinois Infantry, 22
6th Illinois Cavalry, 29
6th Tennessee Cavalry (U.S.)
    Company A, 17, 18, 32, 90
    Company B, 17
    Company C, 17
    Company D, 17, 65
    Company E, 17, 76, 83
    Company F, 17
    Company G, 7, 18, 80, 83
    Company H, 46, 82
    Company I, 44, 48
    Company K, 43, 44
    Company L, 44
    Company M, 44, 81, 83
    designated as, 44
    motto, 17

7

7th Illinois Cavalry, 47
7th Kansas Cavalry, 47
7th Mississippi Cavalry, 30
7th Tennessee Cavalry (U.S.), 48, 74

9

9th Illinois Cavalry, 47
9th Illinois Cavalry (U.S.), 47
9th Illinois Infantry (U.S.), 38
9th llinois Cavalry, 46

A

Alien Enemies Act, 5
Andersonville, GA, 74, 122, 135
Arkansas, 18

B

Battle of King's Mountain, 9
Bell, Job, 118
Bell, John, 80, 90, 97, 118, 132
Berry, Joseph G., 109, 120
Bethel Station, TN, 15, 17, 18, 20, 31,
    36, 121, 123, 125
Bills, John H., 3, 72, 73, 131
Blackburn, G.W., 91
Bloomfield, MO, 122
Boatman, James L.W., 65, 91, 102

Bolivar, TN, 2, 3, 20, 21, 22, 28, 29, 30, 31, 32, 35, 37, 38, 50, 70, 71, 72, 73, 75, 76, 81, 117, 120, 122, 123, 124
Bond, Mr., 64
Bondurant, Churchill E., 114, 119
Boswell, Thomas H., 44, 46, 118, 119, 132
Bradford, Lionel, 69, 77
Bragg, Braxton, 42
Brayman, Mason, iv, 21, 22, 28, 29, 30, 37, 121
  on Hurst, 21
Breckenridge, William K.M., 23, 37, 39, 40, 48, 119, 132
  on looting in Jackson, TN, 39
Brownlow, William G., iv, 21, 85, 86, 87, 88, 89, 90, 91, 123, 131, 135
Brownsville, TN, 38, 43, 65, 66
Buford, N.B., 76
Byhalia, MS, 47

C

Cairo, IL, 37, 125
Cameron, Simon, 3
Carroll County, TN, 4, 5
Cartmell, Robert H., 38, 41
Chalmers, James R., 47, 73
Chandler, William, 80, 119, 120
Charleston, SC, 122
Chattanooga, TN, 70
Cheirs, Nathaniel
  and Hurst, 42
Cheshier, Pitser M., 6
Chester County, TN, 9
Chester, Bob, 64
Claiborne County, TN, 8
Clayton Station, MS, 19
Clifton, James W., 6
Clifton, TN, 23, 123
Coffin, Charles C., 10, 13
Collierville, TN, 47
Columbia, SC, 122
Columbia, TN, 43, 82, 137
Columbus, KY, 13, 66
Company A (6th Tennessee), 1, 22, 123, 124
Company B (6th Tennessee), 121
Company D (6th Tennessee), 118
Company E (6th Tennessee), 77, 122

Company G (6th Tennessee), 1, 120
Company H (6th Tennessee), 120
Company I (6th Tennessee), 48, 74, 80, 124, 126
Company K (6th Tennessee), 43, 44
Company L (6th Tennessee), 74, 75
Company M (6th Tennessee), 73, 74, 122
Confederate District Court of TN, 12
Cook, Albert, 43, 44, 102
Corinth, MS, 11, 18, 19, 45, 48
Cornyn, Florence M., 82
Cox, N.N., 38
Cross, Richard, 2
Crump Landing, TN, 14

D

Davis= Mill, MS, 46
Davis, Jefferson, 42, 77
Decatur County, TN, 4, 90
Decaturville, TN, 6
Deford, James E., 120
Deford, Risden D., 32, 46, 82, 109, 120
Denham, James, 75
Dibrell, George G., 23
Dickerson, Daniel I., 17
District of Corinth, 19
District of Jackson, 19
Dodds, Willis
  murdered, 67
Dodge, Grenville M., 14, 15, 48, 136
Dresden, TN, 44, 75, 118, 119, 121, 122
Duckworth, W.L., 74

E

Edgefield, TN, 81
Edwards, John H., 44
Emerson, Daniel M., iv, 21, 22, 28, 105, 113, 121, 132
Estanaula, TN, 50
Estenaula, TN, 70
Etheridge, Emerson, 4
Ezell, Thomas, 74

F

Finger, TN, 122
Fish, Stephen W., 18

Florence, AL, 82, 120
Forked Deer River, 38, 64
Forrest, Jesse A., 38
Forrest, Nathan B., 22
Forrest, Nathan Bedford, iv, vi, 22, 23,
    34, 36, 42, 49, 50, 51, 62, 66, 67, 68,
    69, 70, 71, 72, 73, 74, 75, 76, 77, 93,
    94, 134, 136, 137
  on Hurst, 66
Fort Donelson, 13, 21
Fort Henry, 13
Fort Henry, TN, 78
Fort Pickens, 2
Fort Pillow, TN, 68, 76, 77
Fort Sumter, 2, 3
Franchise Law (1865), 86

G

Galloway, Robert, 34
Gibson County, TN, 68
Giles County, TN, 82
Gillem, Alvin C., 78, 79
Goshen, NY, 81
Grand Army of the Republic, 123
Grand Junction, TN, 29, 30, 48, 81, 88,
    119
Granger, Gordon, 25
Grant, Ulysses S., 16, 19, 20, 26, 62, 63,
    92, 137
Gray, Morgan L., 83
Green, James U., 42
  on Hurst, 31
Greirson, Benjamin H., 76
Grierson, Benjamin H., iv, 37, 63, 64, 67,
    70, 71, 72, 76
Guerillas, 27
Guerrillas, 24, 25, 26, 27, 28, 29, 30, 31,
    33, 34, 41, 45, 48, 63, 82, 87, 94, 95,
    96
Gwin, William, 14

H

Halleck, Henry W., 26
Hardeman County, TN, 18, 86
Hardin County, TN, 4, 5, 6, 27, 82, 86,
    87, 90, 101, 120, 136
Harris, Isham G., 1, 3, 4, 5, 13, 107
Hatch, Edward, 37, 38, 40, 47, 79

and looting at Jackson, TN, 38
Hatchie River, 31, 50, 70
Havana, IL, 124
Hawkins, Issac R., 4, 19, 44, 49, 74, 77,
    101, 104
Haynie, Isham N., 18
Haywood County, TN, 26, 31, 66
Helena, AR, 76
Henderson County, TN, 4, 5, 16, 67,
    90
Hickman County, TN, 90
Hodges, Elijah J., 48, 121
Hodges, Harry, 17, 32, 121
Hodges, Horry, 121
Hoffman, 44
Holly Springs, MS, 46, 47
Holt, William C., 44, 74, 122, 132
Hood, John Bell, 80
Huddleston, Thomas, 9
Hughes, William C., 5, 6, 11, 12, 18, 27
Hughes, Winnie, 27
Humboldt, TN, 22
Humphreys, West H., 12
Humphreys, West W., 12
Huntingdon, TN, 4
Hurlbut, Stephen A., iv, 19, 25, 27, 48,
    49, 50, 69
Hurst Nation, 9, 134, 135
Hurst, Ab, 10
Hurst, Arthur, 9
Hurst, Elijah, 8, 9
Hurst, Elza, 68
  son murdered, 68
Hurst, Fielding, 3, 5, 8, 9, 11, 13, 14,
    16, 17, 43, 66, 67, 69, 76, 88, 91, 92,
    93, 95, 96, 118, 119, 122, 124, 126,
    134, 135
  and Bolivar flight, 72
  and McNairy County Convention
    (1861), 2
  and slavery, 10
  and Sol Street, 29
  arrested, 11
  as circuit judge, 90
  as state senator, 86
  as tax collector, 92
  background, 8
  burns Jackson, TN, 65
  burns Purdy, TN, 36

captured, 32
commissioned, 16
court martial, 76
described, 8, 12, 14
escapes of, 13
family leader, 9
Forrest on, 77
Hatch on, 79
imprisoned, 12
kills John A. Wharton, 41
on looting in Jackson, TN, 39
postwar life, 91
reasons for Unionist stand, 9
resigns, 80
roving commission, 63
servants of, 10
shows mercy, 43
with women, 43
Hurst, Flora, 92
Hurst, John "Mill Creek", 10
Hurst, Levi, 17, 122
Hurst, Lloyd (slave), 10
Hurst, Margaret (Breeding), 8
Hurst, Melocky (Huddleston), 8, 92
Hurst, Melocky (Huddleston), 36
Hurst, Sam (slave), 10
Hurst, William
    murdered, 68
Hurst. David, 9

I

Independent partisan rangers. See
    Guerrillas. See Guerrillas
Island No. 10, 7

J

Jackson, TN, 22, 23, 37, 38, 39, 41, 45,
    47, 49, 64, 65, 66, 67, 70, 72, 79, 101,
    102, 131, 133, 134, 137
    extorted by Hurst, 64
Jamison, 31
John Hallum, 50, 93
Johnson, Andrew, 3, 13, 16, 17, 19, 21,
    35, 44, 45, 48, 49, 65, 77, 78, 81, 82,
    85, 87, 88, 89, 90, 100, 104, 124, 125,
    126, 131, 136
Johnson, Richard W., 82
Johnston, Albert S., 4

Johnston, John, 73
Johnston, Joseph E., 43
Jonesborough, MS, 30
Joseph A. Mower, 50

K

Kemp, Nathan M.D., 101, 123
Kemp, Nathan Mc., iv, 6, 90
Kemp, Nathan McD., 6, 17
Kimball, Nathan, 36, 37
King, Jackson J., 6
Kirk, 18
Knife, Joseph H., 80

L

La Grange, TN, 29
Lacefield, M.V., 6
LaGrange, TN, 37, 44, 46, 47, 48, 126
Lauderdale County, AL, 82, 120, 137
Lawler, Michael K., 19, 31
Lawrence County, TN, 87
Lawrence, Henry M., 74, 75
Leaming, Mack J., 77
Lee, Stephen D., 33
Leonidas Polk, 51
Lewis, 32, 33
Lewis, Samuel, 39, 40, 90, 101, 102,
    123, 124, 132
Lexington, TN, 23, 38
Lincoln, Abraham, 1, 2, 3, 13, 44, 85,
    87, 88, 135
Linden, TN, 37
Lindsay, A.J., 15
Little Clear Run Creek, TN, 73
Locke, 41
Lockhart=s Mill, TN, 46
Logan, John A., 20

M

Macon, GA, 122
Magnum, James A., 81
Martin, Pvt., 67
Mason County, IL, 124
Masons, 43
Maxey, Samuel B., 15
McCrillis, Lafayette, 45, 46
McKinney, J.F., 2

McNairy County, TN, 2, 3, 5, 7, 8, 9,
    11, 12, 13, 14, 17, 36, 49, 66, 67, 68,
    86, 87, 90, 91, 92, 118, 120, 121, 122,
    123, 124, 125, 126, 131, 133, 134,
    137
McNairy Station, TN, 6
McPherson, James P., 20
Meek, Samuel M.
    on Hurst, 11
Meeks, John H., 2
Memphis, TN, 4, 9, 10, 12, 13, 17, 26,
    28, 33, 35, 37, 39, 44, 45, 48, 49, 50,
    64, 70, 71, 72, 73, 76, 77, 79, 81, 83,
    84, 86, 87, 90, 91, 133, 134, 135
Middleburg, TN, 29
Military Division of the Mississippi
    (U.S.), 62, 81
Miller, John H., 30
Mississippi Central Railroad, 29, 81
Mississippi River, 7, 31, 70, 83
Mizner, John K., 19, 26, 27, 32, 33
Mobile and Ohio Railroad, 15, 22, 48
Monterey, TN, 122
Moore, John W., 74
Morgan, James D., 80
Morgan, Thomas W.S., 41
Morrison, William R., 20
Mount Gilead Cemetery (TN), 92
Muddy Creek, MS, 30

N

Nashville, TN, 2, 11, 12, 13, 16, 17, 46,
    49, 77, 80, 81, 83, 85, 86, 87, 90, 91,
    92, 117, 131, 133, 135, 136
Nathan Bedford Forrest, 22, 49, 77, 93,
    136, 137
Neely, Hugh L., 74
Neely, James J., 72, 73, 74, 75
Nelson, Hugh, 32
New Castle, TN, 50
Newman, Mrs. A.A., 41, 64
    and store looted, 39
    store looted, 39
Newsom, John F., 38, 66
North Gibson, TN, 44

O

Oglesby, Richard J., 36, 45, 121

Ohio River, 26, 70, 79
Olive Hill, TN, 120

P

Paducah, KY, 5, 6, 26, 119, 125
Paine, Eleazer A., 6
Parker=s Crossroads, TN, 23
Parker, William M., 83
Perry County, TN, 37, 87
Phillips, Jesse J., 46, 47, 100, 101
Pitts, John A.
    on Hurst, 8
Pittsburg Landing, TN, 13, 14
Plunk, John Wesley, vi
Pocahontas, TN, 18, 30, 42, 50
Polk, Leonidas, 13, 66
Pulaski, TN, 82, 83
Purdy College, 36
Purdy, TN, 3, 8, 10, 11, 12, 14, 15, 36,
    41, 42, 49, 50, 63, 91, 92, 95, 124,
    125

R

Rawlins, John A., 19, 21, 22
Read, Edward J., 65
Reed, William M., 66, 67, 134
Republican Party, 91, 120
Rice, E.W., 36
Richard V. Richardson's, 32
Richardson, R.V., 31, 47, 98
Richardson, Richard V., 27, 31, 32, 33
Richmond, VA, 12
Ripley, MS, 19, 30, 46
Ripley, Ripley, MS, 19
Roberts, Elijah, 17
Roddey, Philip D., iv, 41, 42, 132
Rodgers, Samuel R., 87, 88
Rosecrans, William S., 19

S

Salem, MS, 46, 47, 119, 120
Sanders, A.A., 2
Saulsbury, TN, 29
Saunders, Lindsay, 2
Saunders, Lindsey, 3, 11, 12
Savannah, GA, 122
Savannah, TN, 14, 120
Seddon, James A., 42

Shaw, C.A.S., 32
Shearer, Orlando H., 44, 48, 124, 132
Shelby County, TN, 28, 86
Shelton, Olynthus, 83
Sherman, Willam T., 63
Sherman, William T., 26, 33, 62, 64, 70, 134, 135, 136
Shiloh National Cemetery (TN), 92
Shoal Creek, 80
Skullbone, TN, 44
Smith, Edmund Kerby, 83
Smith, James J., 123
Smith, W.B., 82
Smith, William
    made colonel, 81
Smith, William J., 29, 32, 46, 88, 90
    background, 81
    charged, 81
    promoted to Lt. Col., 48
Smith, William Sooy, 62
Somerville, TN, 28, 29, 32, 50, 51, 70, 71
Southern Claims Commission, 89
Springfield Artillery, 22
Stantonville, TN, 2
Stephen D. Lee, 51
Stevenson, John D., 48, 49
Street, Solomon G. (Sol), 27, 28, 29, 30, 31, 33, 34, 79, 81, 90, 133
Sultana, 83

T

Tarkington, James W., 16
Tennessee
    and secession, 1, 2, 3
Tennessee River, 9, 13, 14, 23, 27, 37, 38, 59, 76, 77, 78, 90
Thompson, Robert M., 22, 32, 38, 71, 77, 90, 124, 125, 132
Tippah County, MS, 28, 30
Tipton County, TN, 26, 31, 32
Tishomingo County, MS, 18
Trenton, TN, 5, 19, 22, 48
Tucker, Francis, 76

U

U.S.S. Lexington, 13
U.S.S. Tyler, 13
Union City, TN, 74, 77
Unionist
    described, 18
Upton, Emory, 81

V

Van Dorn, Earl, 19

W

Walker, 10
Wallace, Lew, 14
Waring, George W. Jr., 71
Warren, Stanford L., 2, 48, 90, 101, 125, 126, 132
Washburn, Cadwallader C., 68, 69, 79, 102, 125
Wayne County, TN, 4, 87, 90, 122
Weakley County, TN, 5, 68, 74, 118, 119, 121, 122
Wharton, John A. (Dock), 41, 42
Whiteville, TN, 29, 72, 73
Wilson, Andrew N., 41
Wilson, James H., 80
Wilson, W.H., 28, 29
Wilson's Regiment (C.S.), 41, 42
Winters, Fancy, 92
Winters, Flora. See Hurst, Flora
Wisdom, Dew M., 2, 41, 42
Wisdom, William S., 36
Wolf River, 50
Wolverton, James T., 18, 83, 84
Woodward, S.L., 71
Wright, John V., 2
Wyatt, MS, 47
Wyeth, John Allan, 93

Y

Yorke, P. Jones, 74
Young, Alexander, 73, 75, 100

Hurst's Wurst
Colonel Fielding Hurst and the
Sixth Tennessee Cavalry U.S.A.

___ **YES**, I want _____ copies of *Hurst's Wurst* at $20.00 each, plus $4.00 shipping per book. Allow 15 days for delivery.

___ **YES**, please add my name and contact information to the mailing list for news on future editions of *Hurst's Wurst* and other books by McCann Publishing. I understand my information will NOT be used or sold for any other purpose.

My check or money order for $_____ is enclosed.

Name _____

Address _____

City/State/Zip_____

E-Mail Address_____

Phone_____

Please make your check payable and return to:

McCann Publishing
204 Delaney Circle
Dickson, TN 37055

E-Mail: order@kevindmccann.com